Trout On A Fly

TROUT
ON A FLY

LEE WULFF

Nick Lyons Books

Printed in the United States of America

10 9 8 7 6 5 4 3

Illustrated by the Author

Library of Congress Cataloging-in-Publication Data

Wulff, Lee.
  Trout on a fly.

  1. Trout fishing.   2. Fly fishing.   I. Title.
SH687.W85   1986   799.1'755   86–18599
ISBN 0–941130–17–7

With gratitude to

FRANK and MARY VISCONTI
and
NEIL and CONNIE MARVIN

who provided a writer's hideaway . . .

and
to the inquiring students at our fishing schools
who, by their questions,
caused me to put into words
many things I had not yet defined

Contents

Introduction

We who fly fish for trout enter a wild and ageless world. It is a world of clean, flowing water and myriad aquatic insects like the may flies, caddis, and stone flies that change, sometimes in the twinkling of an eye, from sub-surface swimmers to insects with all the freedom of flight. We humans have devised ways to study the trout's home in flowing water but we will never understand its world as well as the trout does. We have catalogued the stream insects and we have become familiar with the effects of temperature and acidity on the trout's environment. Through such studies and with the efficiencies of the tackle or, if you will, weapons we have developed for his capture over the centuries we can become fairly good trout fish-ermen. But unless we understand the trout, itself, and can fit ourselves into its world of predators and prey we will never reach the top level on angling accomplishment or enjoy the highest level of the pleasure this sport has to offer.

We humans have developed a society that is more and more at variance with nature's rules for all her animals, save man. This book is written to bridge the gap many anglers find between our high state of sophistication and the trout's basic and often frustrating simplicity. In our eyes the spider is a simple creature with a brain smaller than a speck of dust but its web can be so complex that few of us can understand its construction. Similarly, a trout's reactions and his survival patterns can be very difficult for an angler to fathom as long as he thinks like a human. This book takes the trout fisherman into the trout's world and examines its life patterns that, for lack of a better word, we call instincts.

The tackle we now have at hand and the strange and not-so-strange flies we use will be discussed but the essence of this book will be to help the reader develop an open mind and the skills to make his own angling decisions. It is a book that will, I hope, give you the basic information to answer most of your questions and help you become your own teacher. It will give you a basis on which to make judgments so that you can cease to look continually to "the experts" for advice but rather join with them in solving difficult angling problems.

What makes the best fishermen successful?

It is their ability to determine the nature of an angling problem and then applying what they know to it and solving it. Trout fishing—because streams differ and sections of streams differ and even trout in a particular lie differ in their responses—is a constantly changing series of challenges.

Only when an angler makes his own decisions based on his own judgments does he or she finally become a complete trout fisherman.

Part One

THE TROUT
AND ITS
WORLD

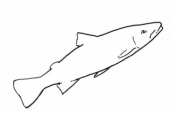

1

The Trout's World

We live in a world of predators and prey; Man has been the fiercest predator of all. When we fish for trout, a predatory act in which we seek to capture a living animal, we are allied with the hawks that prey on the pigeons, we are one with the wolves that take the caribou and the lion that stalks the gazelle. We take pride now in being nonpreying predators and releasing our fish; but we cannot release a fish until we have captured it so we are still as much predators as ever whether we keep our fish or put them back. To be a good angler one must be a good predator.

The best fishermen are born to it. The great musicians are born with the gift. So are the great anglers. Intelligent people without the gift can learn the techniques and attain considerable proficiency in either music or angling but they will never be able to go as far as those born with the inherent understanding.

To learn to be a good predator one must study predators whether they be cats or hawks or very successful fishermen. When I watch Ed Van Put, one of the best trout fishermen I know, cast his fly I am reminded of a cat stalking a bird; in him I see the same intentness and singleness of purpose. There is a concentration on his quarry that one does not see in the casual fly fisherman. I know that in his mind there is a picture of the water he fishes over that is not limited to the surface he can see but the flowing liquid beneath it and the imagined trout he is trying to catch as they lie in or move through their life medium. They may or may not be there—but they are likely to be where he has learned they should be and they are likely to respond to the flies he has had them respond to before.

I hope you will develop a similar sense of the flowing waters and the trout's positions in them; I hope you, like Ed, will become one with the real world of nature, the world of predators and prey and the ever-changing balance that is part of their lives.

Man was a hunter for most of his time on earth. It was only six thousand years ago that he became a farmer, which let him cease to be a nomad and settle into cities since he could then store food instead of having to capture or find it anew for each set of hunger pangs. We have only been industrial for less than two hundred years, which further expanded our ability or need to live in cities and further divorced us from living in and with and understanding the natural world. And what does this have to do with trout fishing?

Because of our changed situation, we have changed our society to adapt to our agrarian, industrial system. To understand wild things and how they live we must unlearn some of the basic tenets of our human society. Humans say, "Save the children first." This is natural for us and beneficial to our society. Nature says the opposite. When there is a cold winter with lots of heavy snow, which are the deer that die first? They are the fawns and the smaller deer that are weaker and cannot browse as high as the big bucks and larger does; and so they die of starvation. Nature's premise is that fawns would not be bearing more young the following spring and that the stronger does will, and that the herd will bounce back faster; nature supports the progeny of the best and strongest breeding stock.

Nature is not sentimental. Most city folk are loathe to accept the fact that every living thing will die and most things die violently, by predation and starvation and not of old age. The wild world is a wonderful world. Man may consider it cruel but it is fair. It is a world of predators and prey. We have learned not to hate hawks because, in Nature's plan, they are one of the killers like wolves and lions and leopards. It is as much a part of our heritage as it is that of the grizzly. Man may have originated as a vegetarian, but he became the fiercest predator of all, with the power to control all the other animals and build the civilizations we have now.

One may ask, "Which is the superior or higher form of life, the hawk or the dove?" This is a question about nature, not about the Vietnam War. And the answer is that the predator is essentially superior to the prey. It must outfly, outrun, or out-think the living prey it feeds on. The balancing factor that Nature gives to the prey is love—the prey can breed faster. Predators have a lower birth rate and must spend more time training their young to be swifter than their prey and as deadly as possible.

Arthur Godfrey used to say that Man was the only animal who killed for pleasure. He had never seen a fox in a hen house, I guess, and had the fox kill every hen in it not for food but for fun. He felt animals killed only what they needed. But lions don't eat everything they kill; they leave a great deal for the scavengers that follow them. Predators kill for practice and want to be as good as they can be at the skills that keep them alive. Instinctively they know that some day life will be severe and

the best of their breed, the ablest killers, will survive
and the less capable will die.

Why do I include this lesson on nature in a trout-fishing
book? Lions and foxes are a long way from trout! It is
because you should shake yourself free from human
thinking if you're going to be able to evaluate the actions
of a fish like the trout accurately.

Let us now consider the trout. He is a mid-range predator. Half the time he is scaring minnows and insects to
death and the other half he is scared to death by bigger
fish, and by fish hawks, fierce eels, otters, mink, and the
like. Of course, no animal can truly be scared to death,
even half of the time, and not go off the deep end. So
trout, like other forms of prey, find zones of safety in
which they can relax. This is very important to the trout
fisherman. A trout, to be catchable, must be relaxed and
predatory, not scared. A good trout fisherman should
know what scares a trout and makes it uneasy and what
circumstances will let it relax and think about food rather
than safety.

It may be well at this point to note the trout's three
primary needs: safety, food, and comfort. His first con-
sideration is not to be killed. His second is to get enough
food to stay alive and hopefully enough to be very happy.
A trout also wants to be comfortable—for discomfort is
troubling and extreme discomfort, such as water too warm
for him to function in, will kill him. A fourth factor, sex,
will affect his activities but with fish that is occasional
and has to be considered only on spawning runs.

To understand the trout we must first realize that he
is relatively low on the scale of intelligence. He is not as
bright as your two-year-old or your Labrador. He is low
on the order of brain power. That doesn't mean he cannot
think. He can. Like the old saying, "Once bitten, twice

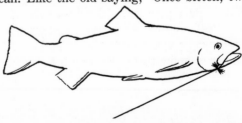

shy," he can learn from experience. But too many people give him credit for knowing what humans know or for thinking like a human. No trout has ever seen a steel mill or knows a hook as a hook unless it has been caught on hooks with their distinctive shape at least a few times. No trout knows that a leader is a leader. He may recognize it as something unnatural attached to what would otherwise seem to be an edible fly—but he does not know very much.

Trout live on their past—like spiders and beavers and weaver birds. Can you spin a spider's web? It would take quite a bit of engineering for a human to create something so delicate and so efficient. Yet a spider with a brain smaller than a bit of dust can do it. If you take a pair of beavers and put them in a closed-in swimming pool and feed them for three generations then turn one of the kits loose the first thing it will do in the wild is build a dam. How much training would it take you to build a dam as efficiently as a beaver with only sticks and mud. Take a pair of weaver birds and keep them in an aviary with only the food they need and send the third generation out into the wild and they will build a nest and use the same special knots their great-grandparents used, never having seen it before or been taught in any manner to make that special knot.

Animals like the trout and the beaver live on the inherited skills of their forbears, what we call instinct. To understand trout you must understand their instinctive reactions. That can be learned through observation. Back in 1947, while flying home from Newfoundland in a Piper Cub, I passed over the tuna-fishing grounds off Wedgeport where I'd caught tuna and been a part of that early fishery. I saw the sportfishing boats beneath me, trolling baits. I knew some of the boats and captains and swung low over them to wave although I knew they wouldn't know who was in the plane. Then I saw three big tuna swimming at the surface and circled to have a good look at them. Accidentally, the shadow of my plane crossed them and with a great splash of white water they disappeared in the depths.

No bird is big enough to pick up a quarter-ton tuna and fly away with it yet those fish were scared of death. Maybe when they were tiny a diving bird could have eaten them; but they'd grown to a size where they need have a fear of birds no longer. Still, the fear of something flying was still with them as strongly as ever. Instincts like that are a part of survival. The fish with such instincts have a better survival rate than those that do not. Lower animals survive on many such things embedded in their consciousness. These instincts, which sometimes save them, can be used to capture them as well.

Prior to that incident with the tuna I had been exploring Newfoundland's salmon rivers, estimating their fishing potential and writing about the region's great fishing. I would hike in to a remote stream, camp there and fish; judged by the fish I could catch in a given time and those I saw and the prevalence of young salmon what the river's potential was. After scaring the tuna I simply waited for a sunny day when the river was running clear and would fly up over the pools of an unknown river at about 250 feet and throw the shadow of my plane on the pool below. Every salmon in the pool would move in fright and I could tell in a minute or two over a pool what had taken me days and miles of hiking before.

Instincts, once established, are slow to fade. In Newfoundland, when I first went down there in the early thirties, there were many harbor seals that swam up into the river to feed on trout and salmon. As a result, I believe, most of the big trout and the salmon used to ease in along shore to the shallow water during the night hours in order to make it more difficult for the seals to surprise them. These seals were a host to a worm that infested the codfish of that area so a bounty was put on the seals and they were swiftly eliminated from the sea and streams. Yet the big trout and salmon will continue to ease in against the shore at night for centuries just as big tuna will still dive from a shadow moving over the sea. It is worthwhile to learn the unthinking weaknesses and strengths of the trout you fish for.

We are still studying nature and have not yet started to fish. And there is more. Trout fishing was a challenging sport when catching other types of fish was simple. The challenge came because the trout's food was made up largely of aquatic insects, many so small that imitating them was a difficult and intriguing problem. The magic in a trout stream lies partly in the insects within it. Some are able to change from a living, swimming submarine to a living, flying airplane in a matter of seconds. Some come to the top of the water and, bursting through the surface, fly away. Some drift on the surface just long enough to shed their wet suits and fly off in their pilot's garb. Some crawl out on stones to break out of their underwater clothing and into flying gear that will let them go where the trout can't get at them. All must come back to the water to lay their eggs, usually just dapping down on the surface for the briefest touch-and-go without giving a hungry trout a fair chance to get them.

These aquatic insects have been identified and catalogued and many studious anglers know the Latin names they go by. But trout do not know these names. They know the bugs and they know which ones they like and that is what a good trout fisherman wants to know. The need to know the Latin names is only for identification when talking to another angler so that each may understand the other. Being an artist I can draw or describe any insect I find on a trout stream and so have been slow to learn the Latin names.

Aquatic insects will be covered in the chapter on entomology, and we will move on to study the nature of the trout in his feeding. Trout eat living things, not grasses as carp and suckers do. Anything that moves is fair game and the scope of their feeding is as wide as the sky. As a tiny trout starts to feed he takes into his mouth everything that comes along small enough to get into it; and sometimes, he will take in things he can only swallow if he chews them apart. A fish has no hands and can only examine anything by taking it into his mouth. This is a point to remember: a curious trout will take into his mouth for an instant something he wants to investigate, something he may have only the slightest feeling he'll want to eat or hope will be worth eating.

The growing trout soon learns that most things that drift freely with the current, like bits of wood and leaf and other debris, have no nutritional value; he learns to let them drift on by, saving his energy for what will nourish him. A trout must get enough food to make up for the energy he expends in getting it. But a good predator will have an extra supply of energy for emergencies and to spend, sometimes, out of the pure joy of living or in practice to build strengths and skills against the competition or hard times to come. This trait will be developed later when we study where trout lie in order to minimize the effort required to get their food.

Many of us who fish for brook trout have been lucky enough to see one come out of the water in a clean leap and, descending head first, take our fly on his return to the water instead of coming up to get it from below. What we have seen is sheer exuberance, and pride in a skillful maneuver. I have seen the same thing with a rare salmon. Why does it happen? Is it showing off because in earlier feeding the fish has gained so much energy for the effort he's put into it that he has energy to spare? Is it to show off for his own satisfaction or for another trout that might be there to see? Fish are keenly aware of other fish. And they are highly competitive. If I get a particularly savage strike at my fly my first thought is that there may be another (or other) trout close by and my trout raced to get there first.

Curiosity and jealousy are both present. How many times have I seen one trout follow another that was hooked until my presence was definitely determined as dangerous? It was probably because the following fish thought the hooked one had a morsel too big to handle and that he, the second fish, might muscle in and get a share. This happens often with bass. A bass hooked on a plug that stays outside the fish's mouth will be followed by another who will strike at the plug to take it away, occasionally being hooked and landed, both fish attached to the same multiple-hooked lure. This competitiveness is true with trout. It is true with bass. It is true with seagulls and with practically all predators.

Feeding the trout in our ponds one sees their competition and jealousy. When I throw out a handful of pellets they rush swiftly to get those they can see before the other fish do. However, if I throw pellets in one at a time when they're hungry they'll rush for them at top speed to get there ahead of the other trout. Often they'll bump one another hard as they make contact at the pellet. On one occasion two trout came to the pellet from opposite directions and the twelve incher's head drove right into the mouth of the eighteen incher coming the other way.

The trout learns that the things that move, either through the water or within themselves (like the pulsating of a mayfly's gills or the swimming motion of a nymph's legs or body) are living and edible. Motion becomes his first and major criterion as to whether something he sees is edible and worth chasing or not. Motion, either of or within a fly, has caught more trout than anything else.

To understand this better it is important to realize that for the first four centuries of fly fishing only wet flies were used. Wet flies are built with *wings* and a body, hackle (legs) and tail. Trout rarely if ever expected to see a *winged* insect moving *under the water* and no winged, flying insect ever wanted to be there. Yet in those early centuries thousands of trout were caught on wet flies and the early British anglers scoured the world for the fanciest of feathers to make them beautiful. When fly fishermen finally realized that winged flies *under water*—with few exceptions—were unnatural, they began to shift to imitations of the underwater forms of the aquatic in-

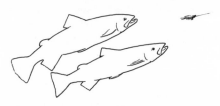

sects, the nymphs; then hundreds and hundreds of the early wet-fly patterns many anglers felt they could not do without drifted off into oblivion. How many of today's fly fishermen could describe or recognize a Greenwell's Glory, a Wickham's Fancy, or an Alexandra, the latter a fly that, stories go, was so deadly it was barred on many British streams?

Even today as many or more trout are caught on flies no trout ever dreamed of seeing than on imitations of the old standbys they feed on. The trout, a tough competitor in his class, sees something drifting along toward him. He's never seen anything like it. But it moves and must be alive. He grabs it before some other trout can get to it. Maybe it is a beetle that rarely or never gets to a stream. It might be a praying mantis, the first insect of its kind in that stream's valley, or a Mickey Finn, a streamer fly of red and yellow and silver, that looks like nothing he has ever seen before.

Picture the trout lying in his selected feeding spot. A few hunger pangs heighten his awareness of things around him. He's strong and feisty on this late spring day. Along comes something swimming or drifting across his vision. He's old enough and wise enough to have a little caution, having been hooked and escaped a time or two; but this thing is intriguing. It has colors in a combination never seen before. It swims in a way that's most unusual. He studies it and realizes that this is something truly different.

But what is it?

Is it good to eat?

What will it taste like?

It's moving out of range and it's now or never. If he lets it go by he'll never know what it would taste like and he decides to find out. They say curiosity kills cats; the same holds true for trout.

Trout will hide and when they have hidden you cannot catch them on a fly. I have waded across the Beaverkill and, stepping on a flat-topped stone, sent a good trout scurrying out from under it to safer water somewhere else. Trout will ease in under overhanging banks and nestle in hiding against the earth or roots or weed growth. On a caribou-hunting trip our luck was poor at first and, in order to get some trout to vary our diet from bacon and beans, I "tiggled" some trout. I would walk along the edge of the stream until I saw a fish dart in under a bank. Then, quietly, I would slowly feel around with my hand until I found the trout. A gentle stroking on their flesh seems to soothe rather than to bother them. When the exact position of the fish is determined a quick closing of the hand can provide a grip that will hold them. "Tiggling" is an old poacher's method that requires no complex tackle, just understanding and skill.

It is easy to see that there is a great deal to learn about the trout and his ways. We have made a beginning. Studying the ways of trout can be a lifelong interest, with new and surprising insights possible for even the wisest of old-time anglers.

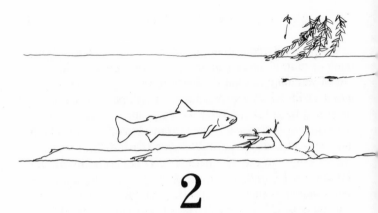

2

The Flow of Water

Every trout fisherman needs to know something about hydraulics, the flowing of water. Trout live in water and it is the water's movement that causes one spot or another to be chosen by the trout to lie in or cruise through. I could show you a great many pictures of streams and show trout lies and try to teach you in that way to find the fish in the streams you'll be fishing. You would be doing it by rote, then, and I would rather have you find the fish by conscious thought of your own, instead of trying to match the pictures I could show you with the waters you see as you fish. See yourself as a trout and understand the waters as they flow so that you can know where you'd like to be if you were a trout. Then no stream will be a mystery.

Having that understanding will not solve all your problems of finding trout for there is so much water and so few trout that they may be at any one of a dozen areas at a given time. But you can learn that in a hungry mood trout will be in certain types of water and that when they rest they'll choose another. Fright will take them into hiding or into deep and open water. When blueberries are ripe you'll find the pickers in the blueberry fields; when a certain annual crop of food is developing, the trout will know of it and harvest it as best they can.

Let's take a trout stream apart, breaking it down into its basic components. The first one to consider is a pool. Pools are resting places in the stream where the water slows and deepens and fish may rest without fighting a current and have depth of water to give them safety from birds and space to maneuver in if attacked by a mink or otter. Pools are easy to recognize. The surface is smooth and the water is slow and deep.

Pools are a delight to both trout and angler. A trout is comfortable there and an angler knows the fish will be there. Water usually pours into pools through a narrower channel at a good speed. This run-in is usually so fast that trout do not want to fight the current to hold a place there. Then, as the water of the pool takes on a broader cross section in its flow and slows down proportionately, the trout will find a speed of current that they can hold in with ease, and they will lie there. Most often the bottom of the stream will be irregular and the rocks of the streambed will create eddies that further slow the flow and make good resting places for trout.

In my early flying days in Labrador I could land at a stream where I'd cast the first fly ever and could almost count on my first cast's hooking the biggest fish in the pool. That's because the biggest trout take the best places and fight off all challengers. The best place is where the current slows to give a good resting place close to the incoming current; a trout lying there can dash into the current for food it is bringing with it, without having to fight the current to hold that position.

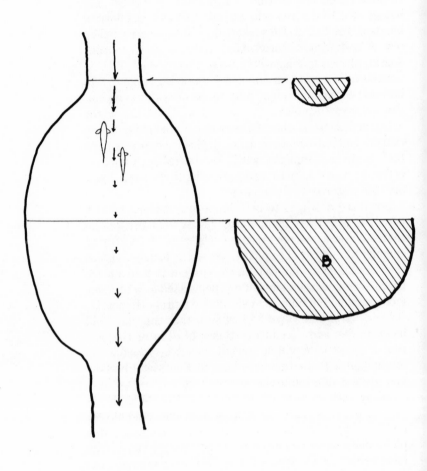

Water flows over a streambed much as air flows over the earth's surface. Pilots know that the speed of the wind is higher when it flows above the effect of the mountains and that winds are slowed down by the friction of uneven earth. In the same way water is slowed down by an uneven streambed. And just as there are quiet spots behind certain ridges and freedom from wind behind buildings and trees, there are quiet water resting spots behind boulders and sunken logs. Normally, surface water does not flow quite as swiftly as the water an inch or two under the surface; and from that point on down to the bottom the speed gradually diminishes until it is slowest just at the streambed.

Dame Juliana Berners in the fifteenth century wrote that the largest fish were in the deepest water, near the bottom. Nothing has changed. The slower, deeper water is the most restful place and the safest from birds. Resting fish are most likely to lie low in deep water. Feeding fish will be willing to work to hold position in a swifter flow if it will bring them closer to the food the stream carries. For short periods they will even fight a hard current when food is coming down in great quantity and they can fill up in a short time. Most often they like to lie where there is a slight flow, within easy reach of a food-carrying current.

Fish, like birds, have a pecking order. The toughest fish takes the best feeding position. Each one takes the best position he can hold and defend. If you catch the toughest fish in the best feeding spot, the next toughest fish will be there tomorrow, having filled in the void, and all along the line fish will move up. A new fish coming into a pool must fight for his place. A fish may have a good feeding spot but leave it to go hide and rest after filling his belly. When he is ready to feed again he'll come back and if, meanwhile, a lesser fish has moved in, that fish will vacate it. Why do some fishermen consistently take bigger fish than others? Usually it is because they fish where the bigger fish are.

Back to our pool. The flowing channel broadens out in

the pool with a far greater cross section of water. The same amount of water moves through any cross section of a stream. If the cross section is small, the flow is swift; if it is great, the speed is slow. And in pools there may be eddies where part of the flow is working back upstream and must be deducted from the flow in the other sections to give the true flow-volume of the stream.

Eddies are the next important component of the stream. As shown in the illustration, these are swirlings of current that come back against the main direction of the flow. They may be large or small; big ones can be many yards wide and small ones simply a little whirl of water behind a projecting stick or boulder. Eddies are important to trout in two main ways. They are the garbage cans of the streams. The water in the larger ones circulates slowly. Silt, leaves, waterlogged sticks, angleworms, insects, and many other things the river carries that are just a little heavier than water will eventually settle to the bottom when the speed of the water drops to normal.

These larger eddies circle slowly and have slow-moving water in their centers where things can settle out. Trout come to forage in this collection of debris and food, especially when the waters are cold in the spring. Trout in

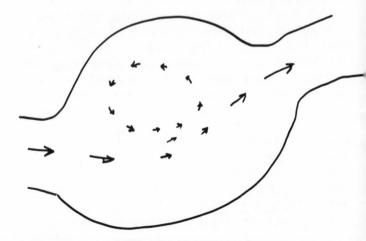

cold water tend to be sluggish and have little energy; for that reason deep eddies are excellent places to fish for them as they forage in the "garbage" that settles there. This is easy feeding. But it is not the best kind. Eating such food as the strawman caddis in their cases is like eating a nonnutritious breakfast food just to get the sugar and cream, or eating shell and all to get the meat in a black walnut or a butternut.

Like hungry bears at garbage dumps trout will gather in the eddies in the early spring or whenever the water is cold enough to chill them and cut down their activity. That's why knowledgeable worm fishermen and nymph drifters concentrate their fishing in the eddies. They know where the trout will find the easiest resting and the most available food.

Not only are eddies gathering places for food but they're havens of safety when the floods come. If you've ever seen a trout stream in flood, you probably looked out at the roaring water and thought that every trout in it would be washed down to the sea along with the logs and trees and other debris it carries. Surprisingly, the trout simply fall in behind a standing tree or big stone or ledge that will break the current and rest in the quieter water behind it. They'll actually leave the streambed and move out into slower eddies in the fields and forests of the streamside. I've caught them there, as the floods were receding, in quiet waters, where a week later dandelions might be blooming. Perhaps it's like having the rest of your house blown away while you were safe in the upwind corner of the cellar. When the floods are over, the wild, capable trout will be right back in their accustomed places.

Eddies, where currents break up, behind an uneven streambed, give quiet places for trout to rest in. Sometimes the water on one side of a resting trout may be backing up against the flow while on the other it will still be moving slowly in the same direction. Most trout lie in the eddies . . . or in the slow water. They are looking for a certain speed of flow that calls for a minimum effort on their part. There is a certain speed of water to look for. A trout will lie in it and be content, especially if, from that lie, he can dash into a swifter flow for the food it carries and then dash back to relax again. One of our students asked me what that particular speed would be in miles per hour. I hadn't really thought specifically about the speed though I felt I'd recognize it in a stream. Thinking about it that night, what seemed to be the answer came to me.

In class the next day I suggested that he go out and study the trout in our pond and determine what their speed was as they lazed around, not chasing anything but just moving along, perhaps hopeful that something to eat would show up in their paths. He estimated it was between one and two miles an hour. Trout need water flowing through their gills to draw oxygen from for their breathing. If they move along slowly or hold themselves in slowly moving water the flow coming into their mouths and out their gills will give them the oxygen they need. It is easier for them to breathe in that manner, I am sure, than if they lie still and have to work their gills back and forth to suck the same amount of water through. It is always easier to use large muscles than small ones and the gill muscles will tire quickly while the long muscles used to move their lithe bodies through the water will let them swim tirelessly. If you can learn to identify this particular speed of flow you'll have found one of the best ways to locate trout in a stream.

Incidentally, trout breathe free oxygen from the water, not oxygen from the chemical compound water, or H_2O. If you take the goldfish out of your goldfish bowl, put them in a temporary container, and boil the water they were in for ten minutes, then put the same water, cooled down again, back in the bowl, and put your goldfish in the bowl again, they'll suffocate. The water is still water and chemically H_2O but there's no available oxygen in it for them. That's why, in stale, low water trout tend to move in below falls or bubbling flows that freshen the water.

A "run" is probably the fisherman's best friend in a flowing stream. The difference between a run and a pool is that the true pool is like a basin into which water flows in and pours out. In a run the water moves through the streambed, deep and at a slow but steady pace. Fish may lie anywhere in a run although they'll favor good lies such as where the fast water pours in and first becomes deep or under overhanging banks that offer good protection while water runs by, close in, slow and deep.

Streams are living things, moving their banks whenever they can. And runs are one of the places most of them move most. If a run curves, the current may well undercut the bank on the outside of the curve, leaving a shallowing beach on the inside of the curve. That puts the deep, heavy water against the undercut bank; there it keeps undercutting in every flood, causing earth and sod and whole trees to lose their earth grip on the streambank and tumble into the stream to provide fish cover, to be carried by the flood downstream, or to be buried in the sand of the streambed and slowly rot away.

The fish in a run will lie in the deep water, which is often close to the undercutting bank. They'll prefer lies under overhanging trees and branches that protect them from the birds—but if the water is deeper out near the middle they'll move out there to lie in an eddy behind a boulder or other obstruction. With a steady flow throughout the run, there will be nymph and minnow life all through it as well as terrestrials like ants and grubs dropping down from the branches or grasshoppers blown in by the wind or falling short of making the crossing. Curving runs are easy to fish because an angler can wade out on the shallow inner curve and cast across to the deep side. When a run is straight, the deep water is likely to be in the middle but there may be deep pockets along both shores; this makes for more difficult wading and may mean frequent crossing of the stream to be able to fish the waters where the fish lie from a sufficient distance not to scare them.

Clean runs with relatively smooth beds are easy to fish.

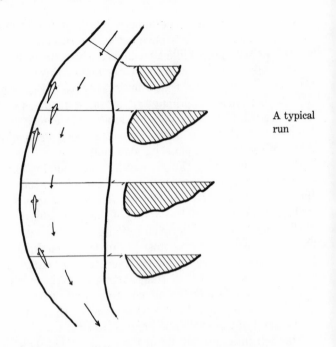

A typical
run

The flow through them is even and easy. An angler fishing dry flies on a slack line will have few problems. A wet fly will swim smoothly and is easy to control. A free-drifting nymph, like a dry fly, is easier to control because there's a minimum of turbulence. When runs are slow they are often called "pools" but, regardless of the name, run or pool, give me those steady-moving, deep sections of the trout streams and I'll be in trout angler's heaven.

If we take a run and drop big boulders into it we'll roughen up the streambed and twist and bend the flow around the rocks. We call this pocket water. Floods will dig out pockets behind the rocks and ledges and if the water is fairly fast it will make swirls and eddies on the surface under which trout feels safely hidden from predators. Fish in pockets live in a smaller world. The ripple of an angler wading will not carry all the way across the stream. Nor can fish see what's behind the rocks and ledges rising above the level at which they lie. Careless nymphs, caught in the swirling currents, become easy prey as they drift by. Fish in pocket water are tricky to cast to because of these currents; and trout, in such water, have little time to look over an angler's fly as it sweeps into view and sweeps on out just as quickly, demanding an instant decision. In pocket water the angler must know where the fish will lie and be able to make casts that will bring his fly close to the fish. Since the fish will tend to be near the bottom if the water is deep and swift, the angler may need weighted flies or nymphs to get down where the trout are. Only when the water is not deep or turbulent or when a hatch has drawn their attention to the surface will trout in pocket water be easy to catch on a fly fished on or near the surface. Western streams tend to be swifter and more rocky than those of the East; in them, weighted nymphs are often the most deadly method of fly fishing for trout.

Our next stream components are the riffles and shallows. They rarely contain big trout. These are the stream areas where the insects survive best and where trout are

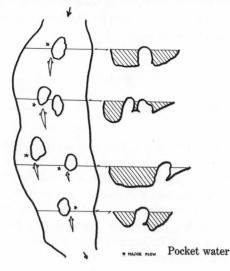

* MAJOR FLOW   Pocket water

at greatest risk from birds like ospreys. Even if there are no longer ospreys, that operative bank of conditioned reflexes in the trout mind will keep them from spending much time in areas their instincts tell them are dangerous.

When we looked at a pool we saw that the best feeding spot was where the current slows at the head. There, where the flow came in and all the food carried by it was within reach of a single lie, we had an ideal feeding spot. When we look at a shallow cross section of the same amount of water we can find no similar place. No matter where in this cross section a trout lies he cannot cover the entire flow. At Position A perhaps a third of the flow going by is within his reach and his vision. Beyond that, even if he could see food drifting by, the long trip over to get it and back again might take more effort than the nourishment that compensating food would give him. Food has to be very scarce in the pools and runs and very plentiful in the shallows before the trout will forsake the former for the latter. Deep pockets within the shallows or even moderate depths beside an undercut bank, however, can give a trout the best of both worlds—a safe place to hide and lots of food close by. Look for these places for they are often overlooked by most anglers and can hold trophy trout.

FEEDING RANGE

A

There are many differences between fishing small and larger streams. In a small stream the trout can see the angler as he passes by. He may fish for the trout as he approaches and be undiscovered but as he passes by the trout will see him and hide because the stream is small and shallow; from fifteen minutes to a half an hour will have to go by before the wild trout will venture out and be ready to feed again.

On a big stream, sixty feet or more across, or a narrower one that is quite deep, most trout will feel safe because of the depth of the water and the space in which they can run and maneuver. A fisherman passing through will only cause them momentary alarm and, as soon as he's out of sight, they're likely to be ready to feed again. Big streams offer the angler a better chance to catch fish unless he's a deft caster and *very* stealthy. They also give good-sized trout room to maneuver when they're hooked and may well give an angler a more exciting fight. But big streams are much harder to read than small ones. The pools are big and there may be several, instead of one, good feeding lies at the head of a pool. A knowing angler will know which of the several lies should hold the biggest fish.

In a big river the angler looks for pools within pools. He can recognize that a great area of water fills the requirement of being deep enough, with a good flow and a streambed that offers many comfortable eddies for a trout to lie in. In which area will the fish lie? On a river you don't know, it's wise to cover *all* the water, studying the surface for any telltale movements that indicate some unevenness below that a trout might choose as a lie. Even the most mirrorlike of pools and runs are never quite smooth. Bringing your eye down near the surface level will usually show little lifts and depressions in the surface that tell you that the bottom rises or drops away. The little drops indicate depressions or "bathtubs," which make ideal resting places for trout. At the head of the depression there will be a drop with an eddy that can make a

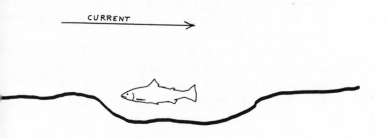

CURRENT

fish a little more comfortable than he'd be over a completely smooth streambed; that small difference will draw him to that spot.

If you have time and it won't disturb any other anglers, it's a good idea to fish down through a strange pool fairly swiftly with a wet fly or a streamer, wading deep to get the best view of the streambed; as you go, look for bottom variations that would be most attractive to fish. Mark them in your mind and when you fish through carefully the next time pay particular attention to those attractive lies.

You may ask, "But how do I really know what the water is doing down under the surface? Underwater currents are bewildering!"

There is a simple way to study and learn the hydraulics of stream flow. It will tell you exactly what is happening at any point at any depth. Take a short length of soft ribbon or yarn and tie it to the end of a rod tip. When you place the rod tip at any point under the surface the bright yarn will move out in the direction the current is flowing. As you move it from point to point it will tell you how fast and in what direction the flow is at each spot. Every angler should do some studying of this kind.

Wade out into the current until you're knee deep. Start with the tip just under the surface and hold it there. The bright, fluffy yarn will stream out in the flow. When it is out straight, the flow is very fast. As you move it down deeper it will tend to sink a little lower as it stretches away from the tip guide to which you've attached it, indicating a slower flow. If you get the yarn or ribbon right down behind a streambed boulder in the flow the yarn will begin to swing around as the water moves it in an eddy. It may even move back upstream against the movement of the surface flow.

Pure water, like clean air, is essentially invisible. You cannot see it move in its currents. But a windsock at an airport and the bit of ribbon at your rod tip can tell you what you as a fisherman or a pilot need to know. By finding different flows *at the surface* and testing them with your flow indicator, you can determine how to read the currents. You can *see* the flow at the surface and make a judgment of its speed. Then you'll know that whenever the ribbon takes on a particular curve it is in water of identical speed, no matter what the depth or what the water looks like on the surface—just as a pilot can tell by the droop or the rigidity of the windsock and its direction, the things he needs to know about the wind.

Now let's go a little farther. You may have to use two sections of your fly rod to reach the places but you'll want to put that dangling ribbon or yarn exactly where you've seen a good trout lying. This way you can tell what the flow is where the trout was. Do this a dozen times and you'll establish in your mind the speed of flow a trout likes to lie in. Look at the surface water above each of those trout lies and you'll begin a see a pattern that can indicate, whenever you see it, that there's a good trout lie beneath it at the depths you've found trout lying.

Where trout choose to lie can be a complicated matter but your current indicator can simplify your understanding. This is just one of the many ways in which anglers can answer their own questions better than anyone else can ever give them those answers. *You* do the testing and *you* know, by your own feeling or by seeing, the answers. When first thinking of this book I thought I might call it *The Thinking Trout Fisherman* because my overriding purpose is to make you think and, having thought, to make your own fishing decisions. There are so many times I get questions that could be answered better by the questioners than by me or anyone else.

Look for areas where the flow gathers to carry a larger than usual part of the stream's food. Look for resting places within easy reach of that food source. Look for safe, deep water with the right speed to bring easy breathing. Look for shade when the stream is hot in the

LEVEL 8

LEVEL 7

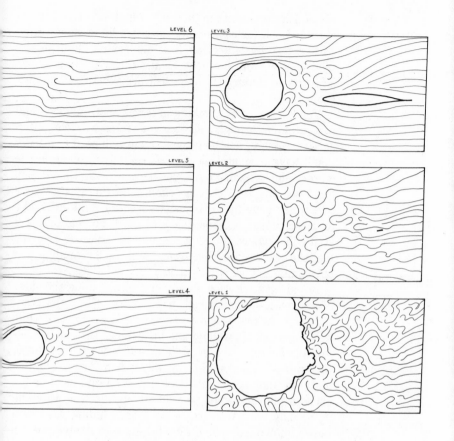

Side view of a trout in its lie . . . and numbered lateral stream-
flow charts, top to bottom

sun. Look for warmth in the early season when the stream is cold. Look for *edges* where fish can lie in slow water, with a fast food-carrying flow alongside. Think of the trout's needs and preferences and there'll be a real satisfaction in finding that the fish are where you expect them to be.

You'll learn to be thinking in terms of stream flow and as you move through a stream your mind will look, often subconsciously, for the places a trout will be. Eventually you'll have a mental picture of trout, lying deep in the waters you're fishing over; you'll know, even though you can't see the fish, that he *should* be there; and you'll maneuver your fly to be just where you think he'll take it. Sometimes that imaginary fish will be real and will strike just where you expected him to strike. Then you'll feel the warm glow that comes with understanding and outwitting a worthwhile quarry.

It's always wise for an angler to walk along the sides of a stream without a rod, just looking. From that vantage point he may see many things he'd never notice while he's intent on his wading and his fishing. Instead of casting immediately to a good lie or a fish he can see there, the empty-handed angler can only watch. As the minutes go by he may see trout feeding in a special lane; or because a bug happened to drift by and he was watching it, he may see a trout come out from a hiding place he'd never known existed. Later, fishing this stretch, he can put a fly to that exact spot and catch a fish he'd never have caught otherwise.

There is much to be learned by watching. There is especially valuable knowledge to be gained by studying the hydraulics of a river, the types of water it contains and its infinitely interesting currents.

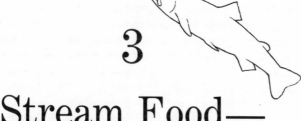

3

Stream Food— Entomology

Mayfly

Aquatic insects provide most of the trout's stream food. They're divided into four main classifications—mayflies, caddisflies, stoneflies, and midges.

Mayflies are the fly fisherman's favorite. They're *on* the water more than the other groups, except, possibly, for the midges which are much more difficult to imitate. The mayfly cycle starts with the egg, which becomes a nymph. The nymph grows and in about a year is ready to leave his underwater home in the stream and take to the air. The typical mayfly nymph, at this stage, rises to the surface, where its outer skin splits; as it drifts along, the mayfly adult crawls out of its skin and, floating on it or on its legs and body, waits for its wings to spread out and dry. The process is similar to that of a butterfly coming out of a cocoon.

 The mayfly nymph has the typical flattened shape, wider than it is deep, of most nymphs. Mayfly nymphs usually have three tails, although this is not always true. They have gill filaments that extend out from the segments of the abdomen to each side. These gills vibrate and flutter as the nymph breathes, a movement which can be quickly seen and used for identification. They live both in streambed gravel and in soft, muddy bottoms. Most are crawlers but some are swift swimmers and quite predatory. The study of nymphs and the flying insects they become can take a long time but many fly fishermen believe such study is well worth the effort.

Mayfly
nymph

When the mayfly first hatches out on the water's surface it is momentarily helpless and is an easy prey for the trout and for the swallows that swoop down from their flight to pick it off the water. When the air is dry and warm the drying time for its wings may not be more than a few seconds and it may not have to drift very far but when it is cold and the air is damp a mayfly can have a very long drift. The mayfly drifts with its wings up over its back, tight together, like a vertical sail on a boat. Mayflies have two main wings, with two smaller vestigial rear wings clamped tightly against them. This hatching and drifting is a great time for the trout and a most exciting time for the dry-fly fisherman. When a good hatch comes on, all the trout in the area join in the feast.

The times of the hatch of any particular mayfly species are generally predictable, allowing for weather variations from spring to spring. It is usually the day after you leave or the week before you get there! On the Beaverkill we count on the Hendrickson hatch coming off between April 26th and May 15th; March Browns hatch from May

24th to June 7th; the green drakes, if we get them, should come along about the first week in June. When there are only a few flies they may be so spread out that a "hatch" really doesn't develop. The intensity of the hatch and the hour may vary greatly from day to day, depending on conditions.

Unlike most aquatic insects, the mayfly makes a second transformation into another flying stage, which is the true adult, procreating, egg-laying stage of its cycle. The first flying stage is called the dun form. Its wings are opaque and it is only a fair flyer. Once it is able to take off from the stream it will fly up into the trees or shrubbery. It flies relatively slowly, with its head up and its tail down, body almost vertical. It will retain the dun form for only a day or two; then it will pause somewhere to shed its skin and come out from that as a different insect. It will shed its old wings along with the case and have new ones. Its body shape and size will be roughly the same as before but its wings will be gossamer and transparent. This is the spinner stage. Now it will fly with much greater speed, often bouncing along in its flight. Males will find females and couple in flight and they will dance in the air over the fields and over the water. Then the females will dance to the water in the briefest of touches and, little by little, deposit their eggs. The eggs will sink to the tiny crevices of the streambed and start their growth as nymphs. When the eggs are laid, both males and females will fall to the water, spent, their wings stretched out on each side of their bodies, flat on the surface, to drift and die. The whole period of both flying stages will be a matter of only a few days.

Mayflies vary in size from the giant *Hexagenia*, which can be over two inches long, to the miniature *Baetis*, with a total length of less than a quarter of an inch. They vary in color from soft grays to yellows and darkest browns. Many are identified by color in their names like the Iron Blue Dun, the Sulphur Blue, and the March Brown. Experience can tell you which ones inhabit the streams you

Caddisfly

fish. Books can tell you the Latin names of each.

Caddisflies are an increasingly important staple in the trout's diet. At rest their four wings lie down over their backs in a tent form which is quite distinctive. In Britain they are called sedges. In Newfoundland they are called alder flies because they are concentrated in the alder bushes along the streams.

Caddis have a very different life cycle from that of the mayflies. Instead of becoming a free-moving nymph, the egg turns into a worm, which in almost all cases builds a case or "house" to live in. Its head and legs can protrude from the front of its case so that it can crawl on the bottom in still water. Some caddis in cases attach themselves to stones. Some, like the straw man, drift freely or crawl along the bottom in eddies and slow waters, like a turtle in its shell. The straw man or stick caddis is very predatory. Often, when we've captured a number of different nymphs and put them all in water in a shallow pan, we'll see a straw man crawl over to a mayfly nymph and start to devour it.

Cased caddis

At a certain time the caddis worm, in its case, will metamorphoze into a pupae just as the caterpillar turns into a pupae before changing into a butterfly. When it is ready, the pupae case will break open and the caddisfly, ready to go to wing, will shoot to the surface and immediately fly away. Trout have to be ready and watching and fast, indeed, to catch these caddis on their way up. They're not, like the mayflies, easy pickings. Most of them escape the trout to fly away and mate.

Caddis fly very well. Beating their four wings in a steady whir, they can be seen flying upstream when they are not resting on the bushes at streamside or mating. They fly upstream, as egg-laying aquatic insects must, so that their eggs, which will be carried downstream when they're laid on the surface, will drift into the same feeding area where their parents grew. When they hatch and fly and when they lay their eggs, the caddis are in a hurry. In egg-laying they drop to the surface and instantly bounce back up into the air again. Trout have to be on the spot and very swift to catch them. The rises a trout makes for a caddis must be fast and are usually splashy instead of the lazy, deliberate rises a trout can use to take down a mayfly. The type of rise you see, even at a distance, can tell a trout fisherman something about the insect that was being taken. Caddisflies are usually from half an inch to one inch long.

Stonefly

The stoneflies got their name, probably, because they do not hatch in or on the stream in which they were born but crawl out on dry stones, out of range of the trout, to shed their cases and fly away. Like mayflies and caddises, stoneflies come in a wide range of sizes. They also come in a wide range of colors. They're yellow and green and blonde but the largest and commonest are dark toward black on the back and yellowish on the belly—and their size range is like that of the mayflies.

The stonefly has four wings, which it folds down flat over its back when it is not flying. Stoneflies are often blown to the water by the winds and so do not entirely escape from being eaten by the trout. They're a fairly common insect found in practically all of our trout areas—and on certain western rivers the very large stonefly, called the "salmon fly," is *the* most dramatic aquatic trout food.

The stonefly nymphs have two wing cases instead of one as mayflies do and they have two tails rather than the usual three for the mayfly. They tend to be dark on top and light or yellowish on the underside. They're quick, and active and hard to catch. They tend to live in the stones and gravel of the streambeds, another reason for calling them stoneflies. Their gills are forward, at their thorax, instead of being along the sides of the abdomen as the mayfly's are.

Stonefly nymph

The fourth and final of the major classes of aquatic insects the trout feed on are the diptera or midges. These insects develop from the eggs into a tiny worm that, in due course, becomes a pupae and then changes into a tiny two-winged fly with gauze wings, much like a miniature housefly. The most important thing for a trout fisherman to determine is the size. All are very small and an angler can hope that the trout he's casting a midge imitation to is looking for jumbo midges rather than the usual size. Anglers consistently hope the trout will take their midge imitations even though they know they're too large.

The pupae or worm stage sometimes drifts in the surface film as it hatches and wings are not an important part of the imitation. In any case, the wings, being transparent, do not show up much unless they're spread on the surface or buzzing.

As with bears in blueberry season, trout will find millions of midges buzzing along just over the surface or drifting on it. Like bears with a pawful of blueberries, one gulp may give a trout many midges. Trout must find them not only good tasting but nutritional as well.

Beyond the big four categories there are many other forms of stream insects, crustaceans, and minnows on which trout feed. One of the common insect forms is the waterworm that becomes the cranefly, the bug that looks like a greatly oversized mosquito but doesn't bite. Waterworms, which are up to two inches long, are sluggish and tend to live in quiet or eddy water. They're good trout food.

Hellgramites are the underwater form of the dobsonfly. They can get to be about three inches long and develop nippers that can give you a sharp bite. They're best known as a bait for bass but they're often found in trout streams and trout often feed on them.

Crawfish

The chief stream crustaceans are the crawfish and shrimp. Crawfish look like little lobsters with a pair of formidable claws; these can give you a nip though they'll rarely break the skin. Trout like crawfish and crawfish imitations often work well. Crawfish feed on nymphs and small fish and are found where there is gravel or grass to hide in. They tend to be nocturnal but are often out during the daylight hours.

Shrimp

Shrimp need water on the basic side and aren't likely to be found where the ph is seven or less. They're most at home where there is grass or weeds. They swim quite well. They're a favorite trout food and will give the flesh of a trout that feeds on them a pink or reddish color.

Leeches, newts, frogs, and elvers add to the long list of possible trout foods, their importance depending on the locality.

Sculpin

Any small fish is fair game to a trout, small trout included, perhaps even preferred. Trout are a low form of life and food is food. Trout don't have a family life although they may, especially in lakes and slow water, stay in schools even into adulthood. Minnows vary with the stream and range from the small trout through shiners, chubs, dace, and other free swimmers to little catfish, sculpins, and darters. Little stone cats, sculpins, and darters count on escape by getting into rocky crevices since their speed is no match for a trout's. The free swimmers do have speed in short bursts and can try to outmaneuver a trout. Their best chance for survival is to stay in shallow water where the trout cannot turn and twist well when pursuing them. In open water, any big strong fish can tire out a smaller one and, when he's tired, outmaneuver him. Minnows in large schools in open water seem to have a fatalistic attitude. If a big trout finds them

Stone cat

Shiner

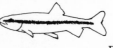

Dace

they seem to accept the fact that the trout will eat some of them and the rest will get away; it's as if they knew Nature had made them lay and fertilize their thousands of eggs just so that enough would survive until the next egg-laying time.

The use of scents is becoming a common topic in the outdoor magazines. How important is it to the trout fisherman that his flies not only look edible but *smell* that way? Not very important, really. The trout is primarily a sight feeder and motion is probably the most important factor in his decision to take a fly. Scents spread very slowly in still air or water. The only time you can smell most things is when the movement of the air brings the scent to you. You can't tell what a flower smells like if it is across the wind from you—and trout can't smell your fly until they are directly downstream of it. That's a very small part of the time. If a fish follows a fly, uncertain as to whether or not to take it, he'll get its scent and it could actually be a factor in inducing a strike. But these times are few. I doubt if it will ever be worth the trouble for fly fishermen for trout to soak their flies in "gravy," particularly those who fish with dry flies, where very little scent will reach the water and when it does will spread extremely slowly.

Catfish and carp and the rest of the sniffers are greatly affected by smells. Trout, cruising in still water or in an eddy, *might* be attracted to an almost stationary fly that smells like strawberry shortcake to them . . . but that begins to sound a lot like still fishing.

This extremely brief mention of the foods trout eat is meant only to introduce that subject to your thinking. Knowledge of what a trout eats, and when, and how that food behaves, is essential to your becoming a consistently successful trout fisherman. It varies from stream to stream and can best be learned by experience and careful observation.

4

Temperature

Trout are cold-blooded animals; their body temperature is always the same as the water they swim in. It is important to realize, therefore, the effect temperature changes have on them. When it is cold their body functions slow down and with it their capacity to move swiftly. With slowed body functions they use up less energy and require less food to stay alive. At the freezing point, they're numb. As the water around them warms up, their ability to digest food and to use their muscles increases and they become more active. But if the temperature continues to rise above a certain point, they become listless and, as in cold water, they lose energy and slow down. If the temperature goes beyond another point they die.

The wiser trout fishermen carry thermometers. These may only be important during the critical times when the fish have slowed down or, because of the temperature,

moved to another section of the stream. The temperatures you can feel on your skin in the air or through your
waders under the water can give you a general guideline.
Because fish are cold blooded it is obvious that in the
spring when the water is cold they'll be looking for the
sunny, warm places and will be most active in them.
Conversely, when the water is warm enough to make
them uncomfortable they'll look for shade and avoid the
sun. Under those conditions, they'll have more energy
and will feed more during the cooler hours of evening,
night, and early morning than they will during the hottest
part of the day. In early May, for instance, on the Beaverkill we'll prefer the afternoons and in late June we'll prefer the evening hours.

Not just trout but the entire life of a stream comes
alive in spring and fades away to semi-dormancy in the
fall for the winter period. In every reproductive cycle,
Nature sets the calendar to give the young of each species
the best possible chance of survival. The whole food chain
moves in the same cycle. The prevalence of insect life
and new, young, easy-to-catch minnows give trout their
greatest food supply and their greatest growth in the few
short months of spring. The rest of the year they may
not do much more than hold their own. (That's why hatchery fish, force-fed year round under ideal conditions, can
achieve phenomenal growths.)

What are the listless temperatures and what are those
in which the trout will be most active? In general the
peak period for feeding activity will be between 55° and
65°. This will vary with the species and may vary with
the maximums and minimums of each stream. Trout in
a far northern stream that never gets warm may have a
lower temperature for their peak period than those in a
southern stream where it is quite warm most of the time.

Temperature changes our tactics. In the early spring's
cold periods we know that the fish will be sluggish and
prefer slow water and eddies. As we get up above 45°
they'll move into swifter flows and from then on up they'll

begin to chase the fast minnows and fight a stronger current to be out where the bugs are drifting by. From 50° on up to near 70° we can think of dry flies being as deadly as wets. Above 70° we're going to try to put our flies so close to the trout that a minimum of effort will let him take them.

When trout don't like the temperature, what can they do about it? Other than seeking the shade when it's hot, they often move to cooler water when it's hot or warmer water when it's too cool. The feeder streams, narrower and with a more complete foliage coverage from the sun are cooler than the larger waters where the sun beats directly on the water. Trout may only move, in warm weather, to the point where a cooler tributary pours its water into the main stream and lie in that flow where the river around it has not had time to warm it up or they may move on up into the feeder itself if the water is deep enough to let them feel safe. Or they may move a long way to reach such cool water.

Harry Darbee always waded wet (without waders) on the Beaverkill in the summertime. It was his way of feeling water temperatures with his legs. When he found cool spots, he knew they were caused by springs and that when the stream got really hot the trout would congregate in those places. As the temperatures get up near 70° the trout will head for the cold waters. An angler fishing the places where he caught fish the weekend before when the river was a few degrees cooler may never have his fly come close to a trout.

Even in big streams where the sun shines on open water, moving upstream is likely to bring you to cooler water and downstream to water that is warmer. This is especially true where rivers have been dammed and the outlet of the dam is at a low level of the lake where the water is cool. Water outlets of this type may come out in the 40°s and gradually warm up as they flow. The ideal temperatures may move upstream or down with the weather changes and the thermometer can be your guide.

The diurnal temperature change may be as much as 20° or more between the cool of dawn and the heat of the four o'clock peak in the afternoon. Checking the temperatures at enough times on enough days will give you a good sense of these daily temperature patterns—and this can help with your fishing. You'll know then that if the temperature on a given day is 70° at four o'clock it will drop at a rate of 3° an hour on that kind of day and that by six you should have a decent chance for some of good fishing.

When the trout streams get up around 80°, trout start dying. Our conservation laws have not yet caught up with what is a very serious problem for trout. When the trout, to stay alive, must gather in small tributaries or, more often, in great schools of hundreds in the cooler water of big rivers at the mouths of the tributaries, they are in great danger. If an angler hooks and plays them, no matter how carefully, they're likely to die from the exertion. When these trout are in concentrated waters where they may be caught and *kept*, word goes out and often hundreds are taken easily—that would provide quite a challenge at any other time.

It is hard to understand why the streams are not closed to all fishing at such times. Woods are closed because of fire hazards. Why can't the trout streams be closed to fishermen when catching fish at such a time is such a threat to future fishing in those rivers? By permitting fishing at such times we are losing the best wild breeding stock we have.

Knowledge of water temperatures and their effect on the behavior of our quarry can thus be of great help to us as we pursue trout—and it can also help us preserve our fisheries.

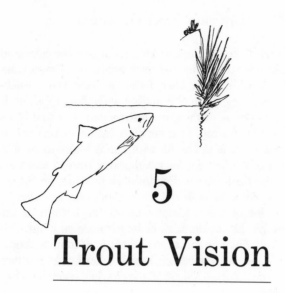

5

Trout Vision

Can trout see color? The scientists tell us they can. Do they see color as we do? Ah! That's another question.

We know that bees, like trout, have eyes that give them the capacity to see color. But we've found that bees, although they see color, do not see color as we do. They utilize a different segment of the color scale and just as a dog can hear a whistle that is above our sound range, bees can see colors that we can't. A flower that looks plain white to us can have a set of arrows on the petals pointing as if to say to the bees, "Here's the nectar. Come and get it."

Think for a moment. The chance that trout see color exactly as we do is, I believe, extremely slim. And what does that do to all the color-concentrating fly fishermen and fly tyers? It should shake them a little. If we found out that trout could not see color at all that would really drive us bonkers.

I go under the assumption that trout *can* see color and use it for identification just as humans do. I'm certain they see it differently than I do, perhaps like a color-blind human, and I am able to live with that. I just hope that my versions of flies in color patterns satisfying to me satisfy them, too, in their own, different way. How important color is in the flies we use is likely to remain a subject of conjecture for a long, long time. I knew an angler who made all his flies in black or white or shades of gray because he believed color didn't matter—and he caught a lot of trout. Color was off the bottom of the chart on his list of matters of importance to trout. It's pretty well down on mine, too. Yet I love to make beautiful flies and, as mentioned above, I hope that my flies intrigue the trout no matter through what spectrum they view them.

Flies are works of art. I tie mine as much for my own pleasure in the choice of colors as for the particular effectiveness of those colors. I concentrate on the light and dark aspects for effectiveness. The speckled aspect of an Adams looks buggy to me. The stark color breaks of a Mickey Finn have a special character, regardless of color. The dark back and light underside of a stonefly nymph or a minnow has to be important to a trout. Reverse it and the insect or minnow is swimming upside down.

The size and shape of a fly are, I believe, far more important than the color—although I can imagine a situation where the color or color pattern might be the deciding factor for a trout in whether or not to take a fly of a satisfactory shape and size. It is harder to determine, though, whether size or shape is the most important. No doubt both are extremely important when trying to match a hatch. In a sense each is a part of the other. If the shape of a nymph is that of a stonefly, how much will it matter to a trout if the fly is small or large and he's hungry? In the case of a sculpin or darter, the shape is the definitive thing. If the trout are rising to little round-ish beetles or midge pupae, then the size will probably

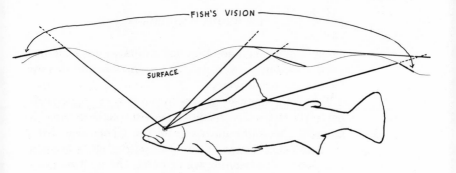

be the most important factor in a feeding trout's decision. To be really successful, the trout fisherman must consider all factors and make his choices on the basis of whether or not the finished fly will do the job.

A trout's ability to see and recognize colors as we see them is one thing; knowing *what* he can see is another—and a more important—matter. Because he lives in water and must look through it and sometimes on into the air beyond where the surface bends the light waves, his vision has to be distorted just as a human vision of things seen underwater at an angle is distorted. The difference between the angle of incidence and the angle of refraction, which is the "bend" or change in direction of the vision in water, maximizes at about 49°. An angler standing on the shore and looking at a fish a few feet underwater will have the illusion that the fish is farther away than he really is; this is because of the bending of the light waves, a bending that varies with the varying of the angler's vision from vertical where there's zero bend.

Water not only refracts light but also reflects it. Therein lies a problem for humans trying to determine just what a trout can or cannot see. I smile every time I see one of the familiar illustrations showing a trout's "cone of vision" as determined by a scientist. I smile because they are always shown in absolutely still water, with the trout looking up through a perfect circle. This is pretty silly because where, in trout streams, do we have *perfectly flat* water? Put your eye down near the surface to glance along it and you'll see lifts and drops where it moves, even very slowly, over obstacles on the streambed. Look for the ripples of wind.

To base a premise on what trout can see under such perfectly still-water conditions doesn't make sense. The moment the water moves at all the whole idea that a trout can only see out of this little perfect circle becomes untenable. The bending water bends the light waves in all directions and at some point in some wave a trout can see through the water surface to everything above it in the sky or on shore.

None of these technical articles I read end up with a field test to prove their conclusions. They don't use a very directional strobe light and flash it to make sure there is no effect on a trout in an area where they've determined he can't see. Small boys, sneaking up on trout in small streams, are careful to keep hidden because they've learned a simple truth: that if you can see a trout, he can see you—and that you can see him even though you're not looking into the water through his cone of vision.

Looking through waves that come in quick succession, especially small ripples, will give momentary images that come and go with the waves like our moving pictures (which consist of twenty-four still images per second and which our eye translates into continuous motion). Great physical capabilities are developed when they become a life or death matter. It is important for a trout to see and recognize danger. Their seeing may be developed to a degree it is hard for us to understand.

There's no question but that a trout gets reflection from the undersurface of the water and that this can and does interfere with his clear vision; but there's also no question but that you, if you make your own tests, will find that they can see motions and signs of danger through a very wide range. Unless they're backed up by field tests, it's wise to figure that a trout doesn't have too many blind spots.

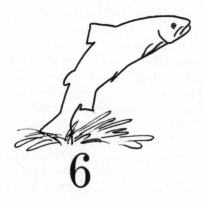

6

The Trout—
Hatchery and Wild

It would be easy to write an entire book about any particular species of the trout we fish for. This chapter will give only a few thoughts that may be informative or helpful.

We fish most for four species, three of which are true trout and one of which is not a trout but a char, the brook trout. The misnomer comes from the tendency of our British settlers to use the common names of their homeland for fish and animals they found in this new land. The pilgrims who landed in New England called the ruffed grouse they found "partridge" because it was similar to the true partridge of England. The settlers of Newfoundland found only ptarmigan as a wild game bird in that northern island and to this day, in Newfoundland, a ptarmigan is a "partridge." The pilgrims found a troutlike fish in the streams and called it "trout." Brook trout, *Salvelinus fontinalis*, are related to the lake trout, the Dolly Varden, and the Arctic char but not to our true trout, which are members of the *salmonidae* family and carry the Latin name *Salmo*. Our rainbow trout is *Salmo irrideus*. Our brown trout is *Salmo trutta* or *Salmo fario*. Our cutthroat trout is *Salmo clarki*. The golden trout, originating in the high Sierras, are a phase of the rainbow. Each of these fish differs from the others in certain characteristics. The rainbow is a great leaper and the most dramatic of the trout to play once it has been hooked. The brook trout is the most colorful—a symphony of red, yellow, blue, and green. But the brook trout is not a leaper. Its fight is all below the surface. The brown is the wisest trout; it can survive far heavier fishing pressure than any of the others. It leaps occasionally but rarely with the wild abandon for which the rainbow is famous. The cutthroat, like the brook trout, is a subsurface fighter and it, too, is generally considered to be better tasting than the rainbows and the browns.

Identification is easy. Brook trout have a white or ivory leading edge on their lower fins. The cutthroat trout has a bright red gash on the underside of its gills—and derives its name from this. The rainbow has black spots upon its tail whether it has changed to a silvery color by a trip to the sea or wears *the* typical reddish side band of the stream rainbows. Brown trout have dark spots in a lighter ring and red spots on a brownish background, which shades to yellowish on the belly.

All these fish in northern climates will run to sea and then back to the streams because the sea gives better feeding than the streams do, especially in winter time. Fish that can swim from salt to fresh water and back again are called anadromous. And in localities where the trout follow this pattern they are often called "sea trout." In Scotland where the native trout is the brown, they are called sea trout; in Newfoundland or Canada where the native fish is the brook trout, they are also called sea trout; and sea-going trout or char of Alaska were called sea trout or salmon-trout. Sea-going rainbows, which turned silvery and lost their reddish lateral stripe, are called steelhead and were, until the thirties, thought to be a separate species from the rainbow. All of these sea-run fish when they return to their fresh-water streams will exchange the natural protective coloring of pelagic sea fish—dark back and silvery sides and belly for a slow return to the natural protective coloring of the other stream fish. Most of these sea-running fish return to their native streams to spawn. The rainbow not only returns to spawn but may make special stream trips on our northwestern rivers just to feed on the eggs of the salmon at *their* time of spawning.

The brown trout, brought to this country late in the 1800s, had been fished for by European anglers for hundreds of years. Over that time it had developed the instincts needed to survive in hard-fished streams and so was recognized as a smart trout, which it was. Two strains were brought over: the Von Behr strain from Germany and the Loch Leven strain from Scotland. In a few places these particular strains may remain. Loch Levens, in pure strain, are said to be in some of the Yellowstone Park lakes. But for the most part the strains of all our trout have been mixed and we find areas where brown trout jump frequently and others where they do not leap at all. There are rainbow-cutthroat crosses with faint red markings on the undergills and faint red stripes along their sides. We've brought the golden trout down to more accessible areas from their high Sierra homes. We've crossed brook trout and browns and achieved a "tiger trout." We've crossed brook trout and lake trout to get a hybrid we call the "splake." We've managed to mix them all up pretty well.

More important than the mixing of the wild strains is our creation of "hatchery trout." Hatchery trout are special. To grow trout most efficiently we needed trout that would be disease free, fast-growing, and food efficient. Our biologists set about doing those three things and achieved them to a great degree. We have been able to grow trout of pounds in a year instead of inches. We've found disease-resistant strains. At the hatchery-rearing station near my then home in New Hampshire, the operator got one pound of trout for every one and one fifth pounds of food.

Unfortunately, when you start monkeying around with the genes, for those you gain there'll be some you lose. With the brook trout the main hatchery strain lost its longevity and self-destructed at about three years. We raised fish that were easy to raise instead of having as our main goal trout that were capable of surviving in the streams and fun to catch. For example, if you walk up to a tank full of freshly caught wild trout they'll spook and run and try to hide. Walk up to a tank full of hatchery fish and they'll come right over to you to be fed. And that shouldn't be surprising.

Of course, fishing for hatchery fish, stocked freshly in the streams, is not like fishing for wild fish. The forbears of the hatchery fish have not eaten a living thing for many, many generations. You don't need to read Ernie Schwiebert's fine book on nymphs half as much as they do. They're babes in the woods about survival. They haven't been fighting a current since they were tiddlers and foraging for themselves. They've been force fed and become welfare fish, which is poor training for setting up on their own.

When first stocked, such fish are best fished for with imitations of the pellets they've been fed on. I feed pellets to the fish in our school ponds because there isn't enough food in the ponds to support the trout we have in them. They're so conditioned to pellets that I've thrown out a writhing angleworm and watched it sink between two cruising trout without a bit of attention on their part. These trout don't care about normal trout flies but they do love pellet imitations.

When hatchery trout are stocked they don't have a very good chance of survival unless they're put into a super stream and they don't have a full complement of wild trout there to compete with. Most of them haven't the capacity to survive—and don't. Unfortunately, love is not locked in to wisdom and hatchery trout breed with wild fish. The resulting cross is only half qualified to survive. If such a cross does survive and breeds with another hatchery fish, the offspring will have a very small chance of survival. The introduction of hatchery fish tends to *eliminate* the trout in a stream rather than, in the long run, supplementing them.

Many states are now coming to the realization that with catch-and-release or other adequate controls a good trout stream can produce trout fishing for a great many people. It will provide a better type of fishing for a lot more people at almost no cost. That's in opposition to the hatchery syndrome of many trout managers who, thinking more of their own advancement, wanted to see every wild trout captured and killed, so that they'd have a monopoly on trout production and could expand the hatcheries and their salaries.

We've come a long way but there is still a long way to go. In New Hampshire we had little or no natural reproduction of pheasants. Stocking them was expensive so our Commission finally voted to establish a pheasant stamp at $5.00 a hunter, to pay for those stocked game birds that God did not give us. As soon as that vote was taken, affirmatively, I moved that we do the same thing with trout and make the trout fishermen who took home the expensive hatchery fish have to pay for them because God didn't provide them and they were provided mainly by deer hunters, bass fishermen, and all those—not necessarily trout fishermen—who bought licenses. People wouldn't have bought enough trout-hatchery-fish stamps to keep the hatcheries going at their accustomed rate. Some hatchery men might lose their jobs but the Department would save money. When the vote was called,

I stood alone. Perhaps some day that sort of thing will come to pass.

Catching trout is a sport. Eating them is not. It is time we decided whether our aim in providing trout fishing is for sport or food or to give trout fishermen a choice. It would be reasonable to require a special stamp for all the fishermen who want to catch and take home hatchery fish. It would mean that all hatchery fish would be fin clipped or marked for identification. They wouldn't be stocked in streams that have a good trout production capacity. Instead they'd be stocked in the many streams that run beautifully in May and go bone dry in August. This would provide good fishing with pellet flies and corn and cheese balls and, occasionally, standard patterns. The people who take those fish home would pay for them. We could list the various waters as to type of fish and the need for the special stamp. Trout fishermen in the No-Kill trout-producing areas would pay a regular license like all other fishermen for perch and pike and bass do, to cover the costs of protection and, perhaps, occasional plantings of seed stock. The stamp buyers who paid for the stockers could determine what kind they wanted. We could make them large or small, make them taste like pellets or like strawberries. Depending on their diets we could make them red fleshed or pink.

Back to reality. Hatchery trout can survive in a good stream with plenty of food. The manager of the hatchery a few miles above us on the Beaverkill says it usually takes about a month for pellet-raised fish to become acclimated to stream life. They don't eat much at the start but hunger eventually gets them to forage and their instincts, those that haven't been dulled too much, begin to function.

Humans of our industrial era are expected to work and live by the clock and be on the job from eight to five, sleep from eleven to seven, instead of eating when we are hungry, sleeping when we are tired, and hunting or gathering when times for them are best. We've forgotten how long an animal or a human can go without food.

Every once in a while, because a shipwreck casts someone adrift in a lifeboat or a plane wreck drops someone on a snow-clad peak, we find that humans can survive a month or months without food. A great many fish and animals do it as a matter of course. Some even learn to hibernate. This is part of "natural" thinking. We can expect unusual living habits in the wild instead of assuming that they'll be patterned after our own. A trout can live a long time on very little food until he is able to forage again.

Once the forced feeding stops, hatchery fish, if they survive, will be like wild trout in their feeding. They may avoid strong currents until they develop the muscles a wild trout has; and because of recent memories they may have a greater inclination to take a pellet fly or a piece of cheese than a wild trout does. Also, there are streams where trout are given supplemental feeding to make it possible to keep more fish living in a given stream or to have a smaller number grow bigger. Then they may continue to follow unnatural feeding instincts all through their lives. In such cases the trout fisherman should broaden the scope of his thinking to cover the type of flies and fishing that work with hatchery fish. Among these are fishing the slower waters and eddies where a lazy fish is more likely to be; throwing out pebbles or creating a surface disturbance to suggest that pellets or other food is arriving is a good trick, too.

But these tricks are not true fly fishing, which is best practiced in waters where the trout have spent a year or more in the river.

Part Two

THE PURSUIT

The Pursuit

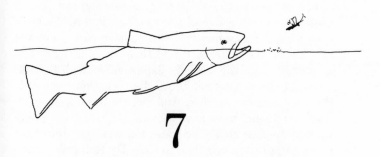

7

Flies and Fly Selection

Without the proper fly a fly fisherman cannot catch a trout. Nothing is more essential to the sport than that thing which induces a trout to try to eat it.

Fly fishing goes back at least as far as the Macedonians in the third century A.D. But modern fly fishing dates chiefly from the fifteenth century in England and France. Wet flies dominated early thinking and the British developed wet-fly fishing to a great magnificence that peaked in the latter part of the nineteenth century. Feathers from all parts of the world were utilized to create the most intriguing of designs. The art of tying such flies reached a high point in beauty and craftmanship—then, slowly, fly design changed.

Two Englishmen, Frederick M. Halford and G. E. M.

Skues, pioneered the use of floating flies and nymphs, in preference to the conventional wet flies. Before Halford's time a good many fishermen must have cast their wet flies out to the water and had them float, at least momentarily, until the feathers dampened enough to sink. Undoubtedly trout took those flies occasionally before they had a chance to sink. And most of those fishermen, tradition-bound, must have thought that the trout really wanted the flies under the water but were just too eager to wait until they had time to sink. By Halford's time a fair percentage of British fly fishermen were willing to agree that flying insects, when they landed on the water, did not necessarily sink. They took notice of all the aquatic insects that landed on the water and the race was on to discover how they could be imitated, which flying insects were most common or most desired by the trout, and when and where to expect to find trout feeding on them.

Similarly, under Skues' leadership, nymphs began to come into their own. As angler-antomologists studied the life styles of the various aquatic insects their underwater forms lost their mystery and could be imitated and were found to be just as effective for trout as the dry flies and often more effective than conventional wet flies. And finally, too, the terrestrial forms—the spiders, ants, beetles, grasshoppers, and the rest of the land insects—were imitated by trout flies.

These trends were followed in America and our fishermen, being less traditional, moved faster with our coverage and developed patterns farther from tradition and more suited to our own special fishing needs. Streamers came out of Maine where we knew that the fighting landlocked salmon's main food was the smelt and that big trout ate little trout and any other small fish unlucky enough to be caught. Ed Hewitt, America's most important early innovator, came up with the Bivisible and the Spider, or Skater. We began to develop flies and fly fishing techniques of our own.

During the four centuries fly fishermen dragged winged-fly imitations underwater where no trout could expect to see one, they still caught a lot of trout. And thereafter there was still a lot of fashion and tradition involved in the flies we used—and they caught trout, too.

During the winter of 1929 and 1930, in rebellion against the typical British-type dry flies, I created the Wulff series. If you were to look at a catalogue of flies of that year, 1929, you'd find that all the dry flies had slender, delicate bodies made by wrapping fine silk or quill around the shank of the hook. They were beautiful and slim. And only feathers were used to make the wings and tails on which they had to float. Looking at them with what I hoped was a trout's perspective, I thought they looked skimpy and hardly worthwhile for a big trout to make a long rise to the surface for. I knew that they weren't durable and that if a trout was caught the trout slime and the messing up of the feather fibers made it almost essential to put that fly aside to dry, replacing it with a new and dry one.

I'd studied the mayflies on the streams I fished—the Hendrickson on the Beaverkill in the spring and the *Isonichia* there and on the Ausable in the Adirondacks in the fall, and I wanted a slate-gray fly with a reasonably solid silhouette—so I created the Gray Wulff. I'd tried to match the Coffin-fly, the mature or spent phase of the Green Drake and failed—so to match it I made the White Wulff. Finally, to give utility to the Fanwing Royal Coachman I changed the pattern to have white bucktail wings and a brown bucktail tail that made it a high-floating, durable fly readily visible against either a light or a dark background. I tried these flies first on the Esopus, then on the Beaverkill, and then on the Ausable. They were an instant success. The first Gray Wulff I fished with caught fifty trout before it became too ragged to fish with. When a trout was caught these flies simply needed a refreshing of grease or floatant to ride high again on the surface.

In the years that followed, other hair patterns were

developed. My friend, Ken Lockwood converted a Gray
Wulff into an Irresistible with a clipped-hair body. Harry
Darbee brought out the Rat-Faced McDougall and the
Humpy came out of the West. Suddenly feathers ceased
to be the only suitable material for wings and tails, or
silk and quill for bodies.

At that time I was a freelance artist in New York.
Those early thirties were depression years and whenever
I wasn't busy with art work I would tie flies to sell.
Realizing that mayflies, which were the most common
species imitated by our dry flies, always carried their
wings together like a single sail over their back when
they floated on the surface, I tried to sell my White and
Gray Wulffs, which were, essentially, mayfly imitations,
with a single high wing, like a mayfly, rising up over their
backs. I couldn't sell them. Even though I'd point out
that the single wing was a more realistic imitation, my
customers insisted on two divided wings. They were pay-
ing for two wings and they wanted their money's worth.

Strangely enough, this fallacy persists almost as strongly
today. The most dedicated of imitationalists, who insist
that they must have patterns that exactly imitate the
insects of the hatches, are almost all using mayfly patterns with *divided* wings; though they've all seen plenty
of mayflies and *know* that the mayflies carry their wings
tightly together as a *single wing* up over their backs,
they still buy their Quill Gordons, Red Quills, and all the
rest with divided wings. I wonder if they know of *any*
insect that carries its wings in that fashion when at rest.
I don't.

Equally difficult to understand was my inability to sell
an early nymph. At that time I was catching most of my
fish on what amounted to the gray angora wool body of
my Gray Wulff on a #10 hook with a few turns of peacock
herl at the head to dress it up a bit. I would tell the
anglers who bought flies from me about my luck with this
simple nymph pattern, which I called the Nondescript,
and suggest that they buy some. I even gave some away

but I doubt if those who received them ever used one fly. Finally, figuring that they just didn't *look* like they were worth the quarter that other flies cost, I put a price of fifteen cents on them. But I found that none of my customers would even think of insulting a trout with a fifteen-cent fly.

As a sequel to that story, one November day in 1972 at one of Charlie Ritz's Fario Club dinners, I sat next to the late Frank Sawyer, perhaps England's best nymph fisherman. During our conversation, he asked casually, "What do you think I catch most of my trout on?"

"A gray nymph," I hazarded.

He reached into his pocket and came up with some simple gray-bodied nymphs tied on #12 hooks. From another box he took some similar nymphs with gold wrappings and a bit of dark material at the head. Then he told me: "I have to dress them up like this to sell them."

Sometimes, at the school, I take out a book on the common mayflies, their nymphs, and the accepted flies that imitate them. Opening the book to almost any page—for example the one on the Gray Fox, which shows the nymph, the male dun, and the female dun—I ask the students to tell me the difference between the male and female duns in the pictures. Only a few come up with the right answer. The *eye* of the male dun is larger than that of the female. Then we look across at the photographs of the flies that imitate them. It is time to start smiling. The fly imitating the male dun is a divided-wing fly with typical hackle, quill body, and tail. The one that imitates the female dun has no wings and is a sort of variant, bushier, and quite different from the male imitations. How can it be that two insects that are almost identical can be matched by artificial flies so very different, neither looking alike and neither looking like either of the almost identical mayflies?

Have I convinced you that there is a lot of illusion in most fly fishermen's view of the flies they fish with? Can you accept that there are styles in flies like there are styles in women's fashions? That fishermen buy flies like men buy and wear neckties, not for utility but for style?

One of the styles that came and went swiftly was Hewitt's Bivisible. It was a round, fluffy fly made by tying a series of four or five hackles on the hook. The first hackle behind the eye, which would normally face the angler when fished, was a white one to give him visibility; the others, behind it, which were what the fish saw, were of gray, brown, ginger or some other color to make a Gray Bivisible, a Brown Bivisible, or whatever color Bivisible one wished to make.

Bivisibles floated like corks when we still had poor floatants to work with. They were the most popular dry flies of the early thirties and a great many trout were caught on them. Then the word got out that they didn't look like any real insect. There were no wings, no distinctive body, no tail. As quickly as they became popular, they lost favor and faded from the scene except for a few of us who used them for fast-water fishing.

It seemed to me at the time that they looked like a fluttering insect. All those hackle fibers created a round blur of wings, perhaps like a caddis in flight. At any rate, they looked good to the trout then and probably still look pretty good to a lot of them now.

Another strange fly-tying phenomenon is that tyers regularly put the most beautiful and most expensive feathers on the *top* of the floating flies (where the angler who buys them sees this first) instead of on the underside of the fly, where the fish, looking up, can see them. A Jassid, for example, has a rare jungle-cock neck feather right on the top, where a trout would have to jump into the air alongside to see it, and just dull hackles and body material on the bottom. It is apparent that most anglers buy flies for their own enjoyment rather than that of the fish.

Jassid

Motion of the fly, within itself, like the quivering gills of the mayfly nymph, can be the deciding factor in the strike. Ever since I was a small boy we've had rubber worms and crickets and grasshoppers. None of them were as good as the real thing and none of them were as good as flies that were somewhat similar in shape but with soft feather fibers that moved freely in the water. I remember proving this to my satisfaction back when I fished with the real things and kept trying to make flies that would work better. I put one of the stiff cricket imitations on as a dropper with an imitation I'd tied up for a tail fly. After a while I reversed the order. The soft black fly I'd tied came out best by about two to one.

Some nymphs are tied so realistically that it is difficult to realize that they're not real insects. They are works of art. Are they too beautiful to fish with? No. Too expensive? Probably. Too deadly? Don't ask an expert. Let the trout tell you. Fish them with a dropper fly of similar size and shade but of soft feather fibers that will move with every nuance of current. If they aren't as deadly as they're beautiful, frame them for your den.

Still another instance of angling inconsistency lies in the caddis imitations we fish with. Most caddis pupate in their cases and shoot up to the surface of the water from below, ready to fly immediately. The caddisfly at rest is distinctive in shape and easily recognized. Its wings lie down over its back like a long tent, sloping from its ridge down over the insect's sides. So we make our caddis imitations with simulated wings lying back over the body. All this sounds sensible. The inconsistency lies in the fact that caddisflies rarely settle on the water and drift on it with their wings laid back. They drop onto the water and bounce off like a cat on a hot griddle, wings beating in a blur. The trout just don't have a chance to see them in repose and can hardly know that they have a unique way of carrying their wings when at rest. It may well be that a Bivisible is a far better imitation of the caddis as a trout will see it than those we are using.

That doesn't mean that our caddisfly imitations don't catch fish. They do. But so did the silly winged wet flies we fished with underwater for all those centuries. The point is that some trout may insist on extremely accurate imitations but that most of them will settle for a lot less. This is borne out by the findings of Ed Van Put, probably the finest of all the Catskill fly fishermen. Ed has worked for many years for the New York Department of Environmental Conservation and used to make creel censuses on the Willowemoc and other Catskill trout streams. There would be days, Ed has told me, when the air would be filled with Hendrickson flies and trout fishermen were in their glory. On such days only a small percentage of the trout caught were taken on Hendrickson flies and most of them on flies that were quite dissimilar. Ed reported that everyone was catching fish: some on flies as diverse as a Royal Wulff, an Adams, or a Henryville . . . even on wet flies and sometimes streamers. Even the Hendricksons the anglers showed him varied greatly. Some were light, some dark. Some were brownish instead of gray. Some were larger than the hatch size and a few smaller. Ed doesn't believe much in the theory that "There was *only one* fly among all the patterns that would catch those trout"—and he works almost exclusively with about half a dozen flies. The Adams is one. It's his favorite. The Royal Wulff is the second and the Pheasant-tail Midge his third dry fly. His wet-fly selections consist of a Leadwing Coachman and a Royal Coachman. His favorite nymph is a Zug Bug with a Bread Crust as a backup. His streamer is a Black Ghost.

Ed's eyesight and casting control are amazing and he drops his dry flies at the very center of a rising trout's feeding lane, not, as most anglers do, inches or feet to one side of the other. It is difficult to judge an exact distance fifty feet away on the surface when you're up to your waist in the flow but doing it can be the secret of success.

It is as important for your fly to *act* natural and follow the flow on a fine soft tippet as to *look* natural. A wise and thinking angler will recognize the inconsistencies common to most fly fishermen and realize the scope of his options.

Here's another example of a fallacy in our thinking; it concerns the caddis worm and its case made of bits of sunken wood and leaf or other debris. Many of us have broken these caddis cases open to see the 5/8-inch-long, pearly-white worm with its black head and forward legs inside. In my youth I took them out of the cases and fished with them on a #16 hook, figuring that the trout really didn't want to eat the cases but were gung ho for the worms. I discussed this with Ray Bergman, who was then a clerk at William Mills, the old tackle store in downtown Manhattan. Ray had just written a few stories for *Field & Stream* and, failing to get a raise of his $25 a week salary from Mills, was leaving to make a living writing.

Ray tried the caddis worms, and then made up a fly he called the RB Caddis; it can be found in his great book *Trout*. That caddisfly and many others that imitate the caddis worm have been successful. Many anglers may think, when fishing it, that they are presenting the trout with one of his natural foods, something he will recognize and accept as such. But for a trout to see a caddis worm out of its case is like your seeing a turtle out of its shell or your maiden aunt Minnie walking down Fifth Avenue in the Easter Parade stark naked. No trout has ever seen a caddis worm in nature. While still inside the case, the caddis changes from a worm to a pupa—and when "ripe" it just shoots to the surface in its flying form and flies away.

Cased caddis

Let me add one more inconsistency. Shrimp in nature are usually an almost-transparent greenish hue. But when we make shrimp imitations our first thought is shrimp as we see them on a plate to eat. Shrimp patterns are consistently pink or red, ready for human consumption. We humans would balk at eating raw, almost colorless shrimp but fortunately the trout take our cooked versions fairly well.

Caddis
out of case

Finally, we think of flies as having to be of certain shapes and patterns. Given a good presentation, trout will take almost anything they can get into their mouths.

To prove this I've taken trout with dandelion heads . . .
and blueberries . . . and little wild strawberries. There
are many tales of trout taking a cigarette butt carelessly
tossed to the water. I know they'll chase pennies and
dimes as they sink their erratic, flashing course to the
bottom; even my pond trout from the hatcheries will occasionally respond to a fluttering dime. Maybe the trout
thought the blueberry was a beetle and the strawberry
was a salmon egg. Maybe they just didn't give a damn
and wanted something to chew on.

Do trout feel they need non-nutritious roughage the
way we need bran every morning?

These are the kinds of questions that the thinking trout
fisherman asks dozens of times every time he goes fishing.

Thus far we have been covering our ability, or lack of
it, to imitate the bugs and things trout feed on. Let's
turn now to those flies that in no way represent any trout
food or anything a trout could ever expect to see. Consider the Royal Wulff. It is one of those flies that, for
lack of a better name, we call "attractors." It is one of
the most used and most successful flies in America. It
may come as a complete surprise to the trout but it has
these advantages: it's chocolate brown, pure white, scar-
let red, and dark iridescent green make a pattern that
can be seen readily in any light against any background.
The anglers can see it and the fish can see it whether
against the sun or with it.

Once in a store I listened to a clerk selling some Royal
Wulffs to a customer. When the selection had been made
he suggested, "Why don't you get some of the nymphs
of that fly. You may want to fish wet." He then brought
out a box of brilliant wooly worms. For a trout to see a
chartreuse caterpillar crawling across the bed of his home
pool must be just as surprising as seeing that weird creation drifting overhead. Wild-colored wooly worms are
truly effective and those two flies should convince us that
exact imitation is only half the battle and our eyes must

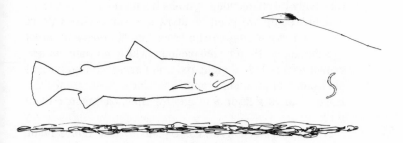

be opened to the predatory nature of the trout that leads him to take whatever is interesting or challenging, however surprising it may be.

Streamers were slow to come into common use by trout fishermen in America and when they did it was with a bang. In 1934, I believe, John Alden Knight wrote an article describing his success with that wildly beautiful streamer the Mickey Finn. Streamers were new to trout fishermen and were very effective wherever they were tried. Within one season, where before a streamer had been as hard to find as a needle in a haystack, there were Mickey Finns in practically every tackle store in the country. The Mickey Finn is a third fine example of a highly successful but completely unnatural attractor.

A Basic Fly Selection

Let's line up a cross section of flies that will give a beginning trout fisherman good and sensible coverage of his basic needs.

Out of honor to the past, and because so many trout have been caught on them, we'll need a pair of wet flies—one an imitation, the other an attractor. One of the everlasting wet-fly patterns is the Hare's Ear. This fly has gray wings, a gray hare's ear dubbing body, sometimes with a ribbing of gold tinsel, a gray-brown hackle, and a gray-brown tail. A dull fly? As dull as most of the relatively inconspicuous nymphs trout feed on! As a companion wet fly we need an attractor, something wild in color and surprising to the trout. We'll choose a Royal Coachman, with its conspicuous white feather wings, brown hackle legs, bright red and dark-green body, and pheasant tippet tail of orange and black. Best size for the Hare's Ear is #12 or #14 and for the Coachman #10 or #12.

Next we'll need nymphs. Because three quarters or more of a trout's food is taken under the surface rather than upon it, let's use three nymphs, two that are "naturals" and one attractor. Most mayfly and caddis nymphs are annuals that tend to hatch in the spring—at which time they lay their eggs and fly away. The eggs grow slowly and throughout the summer are relatively small.

26

24

22

20

18

16

14

12

10

8

6

The third of the three major aquatic nymph forms is the stonefly nymph. Since some of the stoneflies have a three-year cycle of nymph life there will be one-third and two-thirds grown nymphs present in the stream during the summer period—which makes this nymph, I believe, the best choice for a nymph imitation; it should be on a #8 or #10 hook. A second nymph can well be a simple gray-bodied nymph, a nondescript one, on a #12 or #14 hook. The attractor nymph can be a bright wooly worm, chartreuse perhaps.

For dry flies let's choose the one that looks buggiest. Make your choice on that basis. For me the Adams is the buggiest looking of all dry flies; I'll pick it in #14 or #16. For the attractor I favor the Royal Wulff, which is bright, easily visible, and a proven pattern.

Before selecting a streamer you should look at minnows in a small tributary stream or at the edges and shallows of any trout stream. Pick the fly that most matches the minnows you see. Since most of them have a lateral strip and a Black Dace streamer has a pronounced dark stripe, that will be my choice here. And, because there are two main types of minnows, one of which is free swimming like the trout and the other a darter or sculpin, we'll need one each of those. You can choose either a Muddler Minnow or a sculpin type, or both. As an attractor let's choose the Mickey Finn, the brightest streamer of them all.

What have we left to fill out our basic cross section of flies? We'll need a midge or two. Midges, which are like tiny houseflies, make up an important part of the trout's diet. They are so small that it taxes the hook-makers to make small enough hooks and our fly-making ability to make proper imitations. Why do the trout love them so? Why do bears love blueberries and eat them by the ton? Midges seem ever-present on the trout streams. They are there by the billions. So we need a fly or two on hooks as small as #20 or #24. The color or shade may have some importance but size is the determining factor in most cases here. The patterns in so small a fly are hard to distinguish. I'd choose a simple Adams or Quill Gordon, wingless.

Midge fishing is relatively new in the sport. Back in the thirties it was a rare fly-making material catalog that offered hooks smaller than #14. I used to send to England to get #18s and #20s. Late in the 1930s Vince Marinaro wrote articles and then a book about the tiny flies he was having success with on his wonderful home stream, the Letort in Pennsylvania. This was part of a maturing of trout fishing in America; we made real studies of what food was available in our trout streams and studied the life cycles of all the aquatic insects. Before that time few anglers knew that trout fed so much on midges. They saw the tiny dimples of a midge-feeding trout and thought they were only minnows because the rises were so small. We have come a long, long way.

A good selection of terrestrial imitations, for grasshoppers, ants, beetles, and the like, is also valuable. Choose those that best imitate the land-bred insects common to your region. Remember that soft materials are better than realistic hard material like rubber—and remember that each insect has certain distinctive characteristics: the legs of the grasshopper that break the surface of the water when it is blown in, the two little globes on the ant. Think, too, of *when* such insects will be on the water; grasshoppers, even in summer, are usually numb from the chill of the night until the sun warms them—they're more active and the wind is more likely to blow them into the river in the afternoon.

Bivisible

There are some special flies every angler should carry. One is the Bivisible, which I've already mentioned. The next is a skater. I love skaters as much because they are fun to fish as because they have a special effectiveness. A skater is a fluffy fly on a very small hook; it's usually made with a number of turns of hackle on a #18 or #16 hook. It will fall to the water like a downy feather and dance across the surface like thistle down. What does it look like to a trout? I don't know. But it is a thing to chase, a challenge to catch. I believe it will stir a trout to action even though the trout may not figure it's worth eating even if he *can* catch it.

If you are going to fish the western rivers, you should carry some surface stone flies, some large nymph imitations, and (especially for lakes) some leeches.

Spider
or Skater

Some trout fishermen get along very well with a small number of flies. I could, too—if I had to—but I carry hundreds of flies. Someday you, too, may go down to a particular Pennsylvania stream in June. You'll be fishing and find that all the trout are busily gulping down little green worms that are letting themselves down on threads from the trees; and hungry trout are waiting for them. You may fish a while and not catch anything and finally rush to the nearest tackle store, walk in, and say, "Do you have any little green worms?" The owner will smile a broad smile and point to a counter where there are hundreds of them. You'll rush over and look and then stop a moment to think. "How many flies do I need? Maybe a dozen? No! That's too many. A couple should do. No! I'll probably get hung up in the bushes where those worms are falling and lose a couple." You finally settle on six, buy them, and hasten back to the stream.

You *do* get hung up in the bushes and lose a couple there. You lose one in a good fish you struck too hard. And you have three left. You'll carry these three little green worms around in your vest for the rest of your life—for the chances are you'll never run into that little green worm "hatch" again.

I have the green worms and I have some spider beetles, too. Once, long ago, on the Battenkill, I saw trout rising steadily. I couldn't see what they were rising to and it took me a long time to find a foolish one that would take a skater. That was back in the days when we all kept our trout and I quickly slit its stomach and found it full of little black beetles about the size of a buckshot. They were floating like icebergs, nine tenths under water and because they were black they were almost impossible to see. That night I figured a way to tie a fly to imitate them. I tied a fat black body around the shank of a #16 hook and then at the front, behind the eye, I wrapped a few turns of black hackle, spreading it widely like a spider. The few spokes of black and almost invisible hackle would support the wet wool body, which hung down below the hackle, floating along just as the little beetles had. I never ran into those little black beetles again, either, but I did fish with them on a few occasions just to test them out and they did catch trout. They worked on a hatch of something I couldn't recognize or match. They'll be with me always, just in case.

There are dozens of flies I carry that are experimental. I always want to try them out. Not all of them get to the water because the conditions I've fished under haven't seemed just right. There are some old ones in my boxes, like a Coty Stillwater, relic of 1929 on the Ausable, and some wingless Cahills I fancied in 1932 for the Beaverkill. Of course, I have a few last-resort flies like fly-rod mice and little catfish imitations. There are flies with no hackles, flies with no wings, and flies with neither that are well chewed by trout and therefore especially trustworthy. There are some suede stonefly nymphs I sewed and tied long ago when first trying to make a stonefly nymph as effective as the live ones I'd been fishing with.

If I lost that vest I'd feel as if half my life went with it!

Prefontaine

Skaters need good, strong hackle fibers to hold them high over the surface and to let them slide or skate or bounce at the end of a fine leader as you choreograph them to be most teasing. Skaters of simple, firm hackles will skate very well. Hackles fortified with fine, wiry bucktail fibers will be more durable and will resist sogginess. The skater pattern I like best is the Prefontaine, one I designed when our small group of Atlantic salmon fishermen decided to see how large a salmon we could catch on a #16 hook. I put as much material as I could get on that little hook and then added a bucktail snoot. A few of us caught salmon of more than twenty pounds. My largest was twenty-seven pounds.

How big a hook does an angler need to catch a trout? We know we have to be more careful with a trout on a #16 hook than we do on a #6. Many of us are loathe to use small hooks for fear of losing fish even if we are able to hook them. The realization that only with very small hooks will we be able to catch midging trout has forced us to learn how to play fish well, to play them better than we thought we could, in most cases.

Our basic philosophy in flies is to match the hook size to the bulk of the fly. This is a custom sanctioned by time over hundreds of years with wet flies. With dry flies we have had to consider not only the bulk of the fly but its floating capabilities. As a result, we have changed not the hook size but the size of the wire from which the hook is made. By using finer wire we can have a hook with a normal gap and silhouette that weighs less and is easier to buoy up with our floating material. One of the most important factors in determining hook size is the ability to hook the fish, to have enough gap between the body and the fly's body material to get a good grip and hold it. Obviously most anglers have wanted the biggest and best hold they could get.

As one learns to play fish better, he can vary the size
of his hooks. A smart worm fisherman will learn that
smaller hooks are less conspicuous. The average worm
fisherman will use a #6 hook. The best one I knew used
a #10. Fish cannot recognize steel or know that a hook
is made of metal but just as a deer can recognize the
head-and-shoulders silhouette of a man and know it for
danger so can a trout that has been captured many times
recognize the bend of a hook. I knew a white hunter in
Africa who made his hunters crawl in their stalking and
thus was able to get them much closer than if they had
walked in man's normal upright fashion. It would seem
to be advantageous to be able to disguise or hide hooks
in flies that are to be used in the No-Kill areas for sophisticated fish.

Backwards fly

But here is another example of our thinking only part
way. We fished wet flies for centuries and, naturally,
headed the fly in the direction it was going to swim. Just
as naturally, when we tied dry flies on the same hooks,
we put the head at the head of the hook and the tail at
the bend. But our dry flies were designed to float freely
and it doesn't, in conventional dry-fly fishing, make any
difference whether the head of the fly is at the head of
the hook or at the bend. This simply means the fly would
be headed in the opposite direction; but we've never cared
what direction our dry flies were facing and I doubt the
trout care which way an insect is facing when it takes it.

Standard winging

Had we thought about disguising the hook when the first
dry flies were made we might well have reversed them.
If we had we'd have had two advantages. We'd have put
the hackle, the material on which the dry fly floats, back
at the bend where the bulk of the weight of the hook is
centered, and put the tail at the head where the least
floatation is needed. And we'd have disguised the hook
more successfully with the hackle fibers around it. I call
these "backward" dry flies and I carry some to use on
very finicky fish.

Hooks are stiff and a trout closing down on a fly, especially a nymph on a long-shanked hook, will feel it

instantly and try to eject it. In my experimental flies with soft bodies tied on soft plastic tubing I simply used small, short shanked hooks at the tail of the tube first. This worked well as far as getting the fish to hold on to the nymph and would let me feel the strike rather than having to watch the leader or a marker on the leader. I was satisfied for a while but when I was trying to catch very large fish on #28s I realized that if I were to get the maximum bite of any hook I would have to put it at the *head* of the fly where none of the material making up the fly would diminish the gap of the hook. Why I did not realize this simple fact until my eightieth year is hard to explain.

Now I make my soft nymphs with small hooks at the head. That means that they are inconspicuous yet have a wide enough gap to hook the fish; the hook is the first thing to strike his jaw when the strike is made, not the feathers or body, which would cause him to start to open his mouth, and that could let the hook fail to press against it. I can use a smaller hook at the head of a soft nymph than I can at the tail, and the smaller the hook the less likely the fish is to feel it on the take or to see it when he looks it over.

In general, long-shanked hooks have a longer leverage if the pull on them changes from the angle at which it was set. They're more likely to tear the flesh and let the hook pull out than normal shanked hooks are. Very short-shanked hooks do not have as good a bite as standard length hooks do if they are able to swing freely. (The illustration shows this lessening of the gap.) However, if the short-shanked hook is at the head of a soft body that keeps the short shank in line with the pull, there is no disadvantage.

The best possible hooks will have a return eye so that there is no chance whatever of a fine leader slipping out

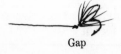

Gap

Gap

through a loop that is not quite closed. They will be relatively small in diameter in the straight shank going back
from the eye to the bend to give a minimum of weight.
They will thicken in diameter around the bend to give a
better bearing surface and keep the hook's wire from
cutting through the trout's flesh like a wire slicer cutting
through a hard-boiled egg. (One of the disadvantages of
small fine wire hooks is their capacity to cut through flesh
in this manner.) Then, having rounded the curve, the
wire will gradually thin but leave enough diameter at the
base of the barb to give it satisfactory width and strength.
I used to be able to find such hooks for salmon flies but
haven't been able to locate any in recent years. I'll assume
it's an expensive refinement we've learned to live without.

The placement of hooks is important for other reasons,
too. Long streamer feathers can cause an angler considerable annoyance if they loop themselves over the bend
of the hook. Matuka-type streamers, on which the long
feathers are tied down along the shank, solve this problem. Tarpon fishermen make their flies with the hackles
tied just at the beginning of the bend of the hook so that
they cannot get caught in the hook's bend either. For my
streamers, I like to use shortish hackles at the head, tying
in longer ones at the tail to give the same effect as long
hackles from the head but without that disadvantage of
greater leverage to twist and lose their hold.

Most anglers feel that a lot of fish come from behind
and nip at the fly; they think that if they do not have
their hooks way back at the tail of the fly they'll miss a
great many strikes. When most big fish want a fly, they
engulf it. I doubt if there's a great advantage in long-
shanked hooks to catch nippers. And any advantage there
is may be more than offset by the greater chance of losing
fish when they're played on long-shanked hooks.

When do you change flies? Usually we change when we're
fishing a hatch and not making the match. But when we're
fishing water with no fish showing we should have a plan

or pattern for changing flies. I don't like to change flies
partway down a pool. It doesn't tell me much if I do catch
a fish right after changing. That fish might be the only
one in the pool that was hungry enough to take any fly.
I like to go all the way through a pool with one fly and,
if I want to try another, fish that one all the way through
the pool, too. If I fish three or four flies down through
the pool not catching any fish but on the fifth try with a
different fly I do, then the one that worked is more likely
to take fish for me on that day than any of the others.

Most of us stick to our favorite patterns too long. We
fish them hard and then, as quitting time approaches, we
finally start changing. We don't give those second- and
third-choice flies much time or chance. When we do it's
often on water we've already fished over with our
favorites—in a pool we've just worked through perhaps
putting fish down. There is no question but that an angler's faith in a fly is the most important thing a pattern
should have, far more important that fancy feathers in a
beautiful symphony of design and color. Once we have
faith in a fly we're sure to catch fish with it because that's
the only one we put in the water. Almost all the thousands
and thousands of fly patterns that have been or are being
tied will catch fish. Most of us want to believe that only
a few or perhaps only one will work at the particular time
and place we fish. If we are successful not many of us
are willing to change just to see how many other different
flies we can catch fish on. We stick with the one that
worked.

Sometimes, when a fly *is* working, change it to see
what another will do under the same circumstances. There's
much to be learned by such experimentation.

The idea of tying flies on the stream to match particular
conditions is both appealing and ridiculous. A popular
film shows its angling star losing the only fly he had to
match a hatch up in a tree and, to save the day, getting
out a small fly box with a few materials in it and tying
the needed Ginger Quill on a #12 hook. The fallacy here

is that he must have known it would be a Ginger Quill that he would need, to have carried such a small fly box holding the portable vise and the necessary materials. If he *knew* or suspected he'd need a Ginger Quill, why didn't he tie it at home instead of wasting fishing time on the stream and running the risk it might be windy so that he couldn't control his fly-making materials? If he *didn't know* it would be a Ginger Quill that he'd need, he'd want a pack horse to carry all the fly-tying materials he'd need to cover the field. Having a pack horse or mule along can be cumbersome—but there *are* a couple of things an angler can do on the stream with flies that may make him more successful.

He can change the color or shade of the flies he uses. Back in 1964 I was making a fishing film for CBS on Armstrong Spring Creek in Montana. We had a crew and the equipment that goes with them. When I had some difficulty matching some very small mayflies I resorted to using one of the sound man's Magic Markers to change a small Pale Watery Dun to something darker and more attractive to the fish. A Magic Marker or two can give you a color or shade control in that it can make light flies darker or add a particular color. Making dark flies lighter is much more difficult. Changing the shade (lighter or darker) of a fly can, at times be crucial.

Another successful tool for "changing flies" on the stream is a pair of scissors. I've always carried scissors in my vest rather than nail clippers for this reason. Much as we love the finely tapered ends of the fibers of our flies, as artists like them on their brushes, and much as we hate square-cut ends of bucktail or hackle the trout don't care that much; and there are times when reducing the bulk of a fly and changing its contours and silhouette will help us catch fish.

One warm and windless August afternoon as I approached the Red Rock River in Montana I saw a few trout rising desultorily, one here, one there. There were a few small insects flying but I didn't notice any floating along on the surface. I thought a #16 Quill Gordon might work and gave it a try. No trout responded. They'd rise a few times, then stop for a few minutes, then rise again later. I tried an Adams and was disappointed again. Then I tried a #18 spider and, after a few casts, caught a trout. Then that fly lost its magic. I brought it in and, with the scissors I always carry, I clipped all the hackle fibers from the bottom of the fly so that it would float down against the surface instead of riding high on those long hackle fibers. A trout responded on the first cast and, a little later, another trout took that fly, too.

Then there was no action for a long time. Taking my scissors again I cut off the fibers on the top of the fly, to make it float in the surface film, like a spent wing, on the two or three fibers still extending on each side. I caught still another trout and just barely pricked another. Then, again, it was dull, with no action from any of the trout, which were still rising now and then. Taking the scissors again I trimmed off the remaining side fibers and cut off the few remaining fibers of the tail, reducing the original spider to just a #18 hook with a wrapping of thread and some stubble, like a day-old beard, sticking out from the shank. It looked something like a midge pupae or a very small nymph and because it was a hot day and my very fine leader tippet was floating it would ride in the surface film. Two more trout took that version before I gave up on it and switched to a big stone fly nymph, down deep, which interested two much larger fish.

A pair of scissors on the stream can trim a streamer into a nymph, a dry fly into a wet or a nymph, a Bivisible into any one of a dozen shapes. It is not easy to *add* to a fly in the field but a few snips with the pivoting blades can make dramatic changes to a smaller size.

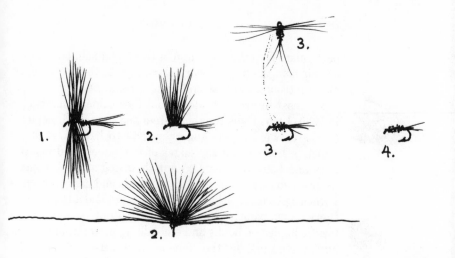

Some New Directions

At a conservation organization meeting some fifteen years ago we were all provided with yellow pad and pencils for notes. As I listened I doodled on the pad, sketching flies. I thought about hackles, the basis of most of our dry flies, and how fine and stiff the fibers were—and the stems, too. The stems? That set me thinking on a different track. Why not make loops of hackle for the wings of an insect like a dragonfly or a moth. They'd be resiliant. They'd move readily. They'd have all those fibers spread out on the water for flotation. They could be set into a fly to look like the hind legs of a grasshopper. Between my notes, I made some sketches and, later on, I tied up a series of looped-hackle flies.

I was able to make moths that were more natural look-  ing than any I'd tied before. The dragonflies had wings that looked like the real thing. The grasshopper imita- tions looked a little more realistic than the old ones I'd been tying. When I fished with them I found that not only were they delicate but durable as well. I'd found a new and special fly-tying technique. The dragonflies, in

particular, have helped me fool trout and salmon. They
are big compared to the normal mayfly but they're within
many a trout's interest and hunger range.

My most interesting idea about flies came to me back
in 1950. I was thinking about steel and how much better
it was to weld sheets together than to have to drill a
bunch of holes along the edges of two sheets and insert
nuts and bolts or rivets to put them together. I'd just
dropped some solvent on a bit of plastic and had it soften.
I stuck a piece of feather into the soft spot and it hardened
there, permanently embedded. So I patented the idea of
plastic bodies on hooks and embedding material in them,
and started making the "flies of the future." It was not
a particularly simple operation to put the plastic bodies
on the hooks; but once they were there, flies could be
made on a type of assembly line.

The cost of a steel mold with six cavities into which
hooks could be set and plastic bodies injected by a small
molding machine was quoted at $800, which was beyond
my resources at that time; so I got steel blocks from a
fishing friend whose steel mill made steel for the Phila-
delphia mint and, with a Dremel drill and dentist's drills,
I made my first mold in two evenings. Luckily I have
good hands. (I can still tie a #28 fly in my fingers without
a vise.) I made plastic ant bodies on #12 and #14 hooks,
I made streamer bodies on various larger hooks. I made
wet flies and bass bugs. I made a long body on a streamer
hook with a stub for a parachute type hackle at the head.
This was for my Surface Stone Fly, which was the first
salmon fly to float in the surface film. It has enabled me

Surface stonefly

to catch salmon behind anglers fishing with conventional flies.

The public wasn't ready for a radical change in flies at that time. Plastic turned them off. Some people said they weren't really flies, Some wondered whether they were *legal* in a fly-only area. Basically, I'm an artist rather than a business man and I was already very busy making films and writing. When all my molds were lost in a flood I let the "flies of the future" slide.

There were a few repercussions. The members of the Grande Romaine Salmon Club, which had caught more fish on the Surface Stone Fly than any other since they'd been using it, tried to have that pattern tied conventionally with thread and wool and bucktail; but it didn't work as well as the original flies they still had. So I made new molds and during the period they were in high school each of my stepsons took over the making of the Surface Stone Flies for that club and some other buyers, making money for things like model airplanes, bikes, and motorcycles.

Sculpin-Darter

A few years ago when I patented the "Triangle Taper" type of fly line and we decided to market it ourselves, we decided to try again with the no-thread, no-tying plastic bodied flies with materials embedded into a permanent body. They're tough. You can hang a fifty-pound weight on the Fish Hair in our barracuda fly and it won't pull out. There are dry flies, streamers, and a growing range of patterns available, each one requiring a special mold for the making of the bodies. Bodies and solvents are available for fly tyers along with the required solvent and the fun of putting any material you want on a fly at any angle is now open to anyone.

Other innovations will follow in fly-tying design and construction. We have an immense number of new materials available to us today and as we study the behavior of trout more and more, and particularly their eating habits, there are few limits on where imagination will take us.

8

Tackle

Line is the most important part of the fly casting tackle. Back in 1941, when I was pioneering the taking of big salmon on featherweight rods, there were many statements made that there was a certain minimum rod length and strength required to take a salmon. I decided to settle the argument and by casting by hand without a rod I hooked a ten-pound Atlantic salmon and played it directly from the reel, which I held in one hand while reeling with the other. This made people realize that well-designed small, light rods would cast a long way and that big fish could be played with them. It established the importance of the line as compared with the rod or the reel.

Fly casting differs from such other types of casting as spinning and bait casting in that the fly is essentially weightless. The others depend upon the weight of the lure to pull out a very light line by its momentum. I can throw a bait-casting or spinning lure almost as far as I can cast it. I can't throw a feather worth a darn. It is the weight of the line that makes fly casting possible. That weight is distributed throughout the fly line in varying ways. A line may have a uniform weight throughout its entire length and a uniform diameter. That is called a level line.

In order to make the end of the fly line nearest the fish land more delicately, level lines were tapered to finer diameters at each end. Tapering leaders could be attached to these fine ends, bringing the fly to the trout with the greatest possible invisibility and delicacy. These are called double-tapered lines and may still be the most popular of all fly-fishing lines.

In the twenties, however, fly casters realized that if they made the forward part of their lines heavy and the rear portions light and of small diameter, they could "shoot" these forward sections out much like a lure is thrown out by bait casting or spinning that pulls a very light line out behind it because of its weight and inertia. The forward tapering retained the heavy section or "belly" but was shortened to less than thirty feet of the usual ninety-foot total length. The rest of the fly line's length was made up of a quick taper to a small diameter that would still have the necessary bulk and pliability all fly lines require to make them easy to cast and handle. These forward-tapered lines have become increasingly popular and give us greater distance capability because they let us shoot a forward taper out a greater distance than the heavy belly line of the double taper could be shot.

Fly casting is unique among sports in that it requires not a *single* swing as with a ball bat or a tennis racquet but repeated swings both forward and backward. No other sport requires as hard a swing backward as forward. Our natural ability to throw things forward has given us better muscles for throws in that direction and the forward-tapered lines capitalize on that ability for our final forward casts.

The Triangle Taper has a fine front point and tapers continuously from that to a maximum diameter at (in most cases) forty feet. It has the greatest delicacy near the fish. It is the best roll-casting line because, within its tapered section, heavy line is constantly turning over lighter line in the roll, which is more efficient than having rolling line turn over its own weight. The forward-tapered section develops all the weight necessary to cast distance with the typical light shooting line behind it.

A "Shooting Head" line has a short forward section of heavy line attached to monofilament or other light, slick line that will give minimum drag on the shoot. Such a line will give a fly caster the greatest possible distance but the shooting line is prone to tangle and is usually retrieved in a basket worn at the waist. Delicacy and accuracy tend to suffer with this type of line.

Fly lines are designated by numbers. A chart of the various grain weights for the first thirty feet of the line for the number designation is shown. This is intended to show the weight of the line load the fly caster is putting on his rod for his medium- and long-range casts. It is a

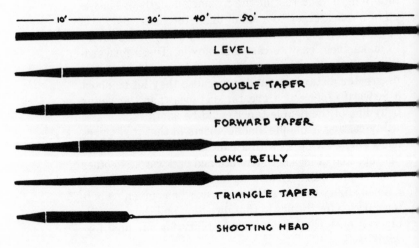

LINE STANDARDS

AFTMA Fly Line Standards. These universal standards are based on the *weight* of the working part of the line—the first 30 ft. exclusive on the tip of a taper. ? and front running part.

Code	Weight/Grains	Range*
1	60	54–66
2	80	74–86
3	100	94–106
4	120	114–126
5	140	134–146
6	160	152–168
7	185	177–193
8	210	202–218
9	240	230–250
10	280	270–290
11	330	318–342
12	380	368–392

*Allowable tolerances in grains

Identification Symbols
L—Level
ST—Single Taper
WF—Weight-Forward Taper
DT—Double Taper
F—Floating
S—Sinking
I—Intermediate, floating or sinking

general guide but, unfortunately, it is unable to give an accurate rating for the many fly lines that have a longer than thirty-foot heavy forward section.

If you use a long fine *leader* it is impossible for the trout to know what kind of *line* you are using. The very light lines do not necessarily give any greater delicacy at the fly but they do handicap the caster if there is any wind or if long casts are to be made. We are dealing with weight in a fly line and it takes a certain amount of weight to overcome air resistance and to punch through winds. A #6 line is a good choice for most people. It is easier to "feel" on the casts and better for a beginner than a lighter one. It takes more line weight to control heavy flies and heavier lines are in order when they're used.

Rods

Rods for casting fly lines have come through a number of changes. They began with solid wood and progressed through glued-up sections of split bamboo to solid glass fibers and woven glass fibers molded around a steel mandrel to make a hollow rod of whatever taper desired. In the last twenty years carbon fibers have been utilized in hollow rods of "graphite." These fibers are considerably lighter than glass fibers and much, much lighter than solid wood; and they have much more strength for their weight. Solid and hollow boron rods or rods of a mixture of boron and carbon are on the scene. Boron is the strongest material for its weight. Boron is not very much stronger than carbon so its presence is not as revolutionary as the change from split bamboo to glass or glass to carbon fibers.

Rods vary greatly in their tapers and bending qualities. Some, with softness in the lower sections, act a little like metronomes and tend to set up their own casting rhythms. Others, stiffer in the butts and generally stiffer throughout, are called fast-action rods. After bending, these rods "dampen" swiftly. That is, they return to their straight positions faster. They respond much more quickly to changes in direction and changes in the speed of the casting rhythm. Casting is a very personal thing. We have different physiques, different strengths, and different temperaments. We need to match our rods and lines to these. I like fast-action rods that give me faster changes in speed or direction.

Small, light rods do not provide an easier way to catch fish. The opposite is usually true. They require special skills. Casting becomes more difficult because the timing is more critical. The fly whistles by the caster's ears instead of safely over his head at a higher level. Longer strokes and faster motions are required to cast the same distances. Also, you lose the high rod angle in playing a fish. With the short, light rod you gain in the lightness of the outfit you must hold up in your arm all during the casting hours. You gain in the use of speed to develop line energy. Longer strokes at high speed can be less tiring than short strokes with more power. Playing fish close in is easier and they can be brought to within easy reach of the fisherman (I once had a salmon swim between my legs and passed my six-foot rod through behind him to continue the fight).

Matching a line to a rod is difficult. The number system of line determination gives a fairly broad spread. To get the best out of a rod you need a line that will load it best at the casting range you want to fish in. With a computer and the formulas and necessary grain weights and flexing strengths you could do it but it would take some time and special skills. Your muscles can tell you which outfit is best. With a range of lines to try out we can find the one best matched to a rod for each of us; or with a number of rods to work with, we can easily pick out the one best matched to the line of our choice.

Make casts with the amount of line you want to cast, trying each rod under the same conditions. If the rod lags a little the load of the line is too great. The line is too heavy. If, when you cast, the rod sweeps through its arc without bending enough and seems too stiff, the line is not heavy enough to utilize its power. The line that makes a rod seem to have the most life and power is the best one.

The guides on a rod are important as to number and quality. The first, or gathering guide, should have a larger opening than the others; usually it is a round ring of very smooth and durable material. The others may be round or an extended loop of wire called snake guides. These are slightly lighter than mounted rings in case weight is a problem. The more guides on a rod the more drag there will be when line slides through them. The fewer there are the less drag—but the more uneven the bending of the rod will be. Nine guides and a tip-top is a good number for an eight-foot rod. An eight-and-a-half-foot rod might have one more.

The lightest reel seats are of cork with two light metal rings to hold the reel seat. Metal reel seats are more secure but heavier. If the reel seat fits against the butt of the rod the entire rod will be useful in your casting. If the reel sits up against the grip and screw locks in that position you'll have a couple of inches below the reel that don't help in your casting and are that much extra weight you're holding up while you cast. That extra two inches may have a small advantage if you get tired while playing a fish and want to press the rod butt against your body to make holding the rod up a little easier and without catching the reel handle in your clothing.

The design of the rod may be more important than the material to some casters and a great many fly fishers are still using fiberglass and split bamboo. Each has a different feeling and action and well-designed rods of any of the materials can give a caster a fine casting capability.

Reels

Reels are designed, basically, to hold the fly line that is not required, at any given time, for the casting and fishing. If you were fishing from a boat or anywhere where line could be coiled on the deck or ground without tangling, it would be possible to fly fish without a reel. But because we move around, wade streams, and, sometimes, catch fish so large that great lengths of line are needed to play them, a reel has become a necessity.

The fly reel must be large enough in capacity to hold the fly line and any additional line that may be required to play a long-running fish. The reel, attached to the butt of the rod, must be held up in the hand while fishing. Just as weight is important in a fly rod so it is in a reel. An extra ounce of weight can take its toll in tiredness at the end of the day.

To make fly reels as light as possible, they are normally made in what is called "single action." This means that the spool is on a spindle or shaft and one turn of the handle makes the spool turn once. Line can be retrieved faster if the reel is a "multiplier," which means that there are gears used to make the spool revolve more than once for every turn of the handle. This can be an advantage, particularly when playing a far-off fish, but it is a disadvantage because of the added weight of the gears that must be held up during all those hours of the casting time.

Any extra weight in a fly reel is usually eliminated. Most spools are as light as possible to give them the required strength and most frames are perforated wherever possible to reduce weight. Generally, in order to get a higher price for his reels a reelmaker must use superior materials (which can give a reel a longer life) or fancy it up with expensive finish or engraving (which will make it more beautiful but not more efficient) or put on gears that, unfortunately, will increase its weight.

Most fly reels have a "click," which has two purposes. The first is to give off a sound proportionate to the speed of the turning spool. Since the fly reel is on the far side of the rod butt and facing away from the fisherman he cannot see the spool of the reel to judge how much line he has left on the spool or how far away the fish is (except by seeing line marks or the line/backing connection). However, the sound of the reel can tell an angler how much line has gone out through the guides and at what speed, once he's learned to read the sound the reel sings. Silent reels do not have that advantage.

The second purpose of the click is to act as a light brake on the turning spool to keep the reel from overrunning, from continuing to turn at high speed when the fish slows down abruptly. Clicks are usually adjustable so that an angler can set the tension they create to a drag sufficient to keep the reel from overrunning yet don't create any extra, unnecessary drag that might be just enough to break a fine leader or tear out a poorly set hook.

Reels were designed with drags or brakes that are much like the brakes on automobile wheels. They create a pressure that the fish must overcome in order to pull line from the reel. This makes him work harder. The trouble with drags is that as the line comes off the reel the diameter of the line on the spool grows smaller. As the diameter grows smaller the leverage of the pull diminishes and the drag becomes greater under the same setting. If the drag cannot be adjusted almost instantly, a drag set up near the leader's breaking point can suddenly exceed it.

Back in 1966 I invented the first rim-control reel, the Lee Wulff Ultimate, which, by eliminating the outside part of the frame allowed a finger pressure on the outside rim to act as a brake. Since the leverage of the diameter at the rim was the greatest possible for pressure, a maximum drag could be put on the spool's turning with simple finger pressure. Pressure could be released instantly. This was a great advantage—as was the capability of putting *on* pressure just as quickly without having to turn any knobs or move any levers. The reel has been copied by many manufacturers since then. Rim control and drags are most important in the playing of large salt-water fish; most stream fish and trout can be played on a very light drag although a drag that is quickly adjustable can be an advantage with such larger trout as the steelhead.

Simple reels can be made to do big jobs if they're handled skillfully. One of the fish I'm proudest of is the 148-pound striped marlin I took on a fly with a twelve-pound-test leader, a five-ounce, nine-foot single-handed glass fly rod that retailed at $12.50 (in 1967) and an inexpensive Farlow Python reel without a drag ($20.00) that held my fly line and 300 yards of backing. It's still a fly-rod record in an area of fishing where strong rods with extra butts and reels with strong drags are considered essential. No one really needs anything more than a simple single-action reel with a light click for trout fishing—though it's always a pleasure to own a finely crafted reel durable enough to last a lifetime.

Because the rod's job is more important and requires greater sensitivity, I use my right hand on the rod (I'm right-handed) and my weaker left one for reeling. All the reel hand has to do is go round and round like a trolley on a track. The hand holding the rod becomes very important when playing large fish because strength is required for a long period of time. An angler's weak hand usually isn't up to it and he starts changing back and forth with some loss of control or power.

Leaders

The line's job is to make casting possible and the leader's is to fool the fish. Originally, lines and leaders for fly fishing were made of the same material, horsehair. Braiding thickened and strengthened the leader and line as more and more individual hairs were added to the one or two at the point where the fly was attached. Someday in the not-too-distant future, we will have lines and leaders made of the same material again. I've had such a test line made of monofilament that tapered smoothly from .007 inches at the forward point to .055 inches at the belly, which carried for thirty feet then tapered quickly back to .035 for the rest of the ninety-foot line.

If three feet of leader is good and will fool fish but six feet is better, why not use almost invisible monofilament for the whole line? I tested it and it worked well and, having only one or two knots where the front tippets were attached to it fooled fish well. On hot days when the sun's warmth softened the nylon and made it pliable, it was easy enough to cast. If the temperature dropped below sixty, the monofilament stiffened like wire and casting it out through the guides was next to impossible. Sooner or later, someone will come up with an almost transparent material that is soft enough, strong enough, and slick enough to make a good fly line. That will save a lot of the leader headaches we have today.

One must ask three simple questions about a leader. Is it fine enough to fool the fish? Is it long enough to fool the fish? Is it strong enough to hold him? Those are the basics and *you* must make the judgment. Beyond that, there are a lot of lesser questions that may be more difficult to answer.

How thick should a leader be at the butt? The butt of each leader, regardless of its length, should *always* be about three quarters the diameter as that of the line point to which it is attached. Leader material is stiffer than fly lines and the bending characteristics call for a sharp drop in diameter here. A large diameter change will affect the smooth unrolling of the leader. We taper our lines to a small diameter to give a smooth transfer of energy and a smooth rolling out of the line in the cast. The leader should be a continuation of the line's taper to give the smoothest possible presentation. If there is an abrupt change in the weight or stiffness at the junction of line and leader, this will show up in your casting.

Our present monofilament leader material is stiffer than fly lines (that's why mono is not a good material for lines) and so a slightly smaller diameter will have the same bending capability or resistance. Mono will be heavier than some lines and lighter than others but by the time we get to small leader diameters it is the stiffness, rather than the weight, that is the controling factor. Most fly lines range from .030 inches to .042 at the point. At .030 inches the leader to match should have a butt diameter of .023 to .025 inches (regardless of the leader's length) to make it turn over smoothly. If the point is .035 it will take a .028 leader diameter to give a smooth junction. Unfortunately, as leaders get shorter with the same fish-fooling diameter at the tip most manufacturers give them smaller butt diameters. Then, in order to get smooth casts a fisherman must insert a section of monofilament of the right diameter so that a finer leader butt can be attached to a .023 insert which is attached to the .030 diameter line point. It begins to look as if you ought to have a micrometer to measure these diameters, doesn't it!

Monofilaments differ widely in strengths and in characteristics. One manufacturer's .005 leader may be half again as strong as another's. Does that mean that the stronger one is better? Not at all. It may be weaker when knotted. If it is soft nylon it will give a little better presentation on the water but it will kink up easier and hold its kinks against your best efforts to straighten it out once they are there. The tightening of the knot at the fly may put a curl in the leader that sets it awry.

Knotless tapered leaders are generally preferred over the knotted ones because knots are weak places in any leader and a continually changing taper is smoother than sections of *level* mono knotted together.

Don't forget the purpose of the leader and be led astray by some lesser factor. A leader is designed primarily to fool a fish. Therefore the most important thing is to have the greatest invisibility near the fish. In other words, it is better to have a taper that slims the leader down faster near the butt and stretches it out with a greater length of finer diameters near the fly and the fish. The final tippet should be the longest. Some anglers like to put a heavier section near the center of their leader to make it "turn over" better. They're dropping a heavier, more visible mono closer to the fish, which won't fool him as readily. I think it's better to keep the heavier diameters as far as possible from the fish even if this causes a slight casting problem and means more practice or study in casting to cast the finer tapers as well as the lumpy leaders.

Leaders must have some knots in them unless they are new and even then they can stay knotless only for a limited period of fishing. The knotless leader may taper down to a fine point, which is the diameter you want to fish with, but, as you change flies, you lose a little leader each time you cut off the fly and tie a new knot. In time this will eat up quite a bit of leader and you'll have to replace it with a short length of level mono called a tippet. That's your first knot. Another will come when you find the trout are shying away from your dry fly. You feel the need to add another, finer section to the one on which your fly has been tied.

Leaders must match the fly they are attached to. If a very small fly it attached to a stiff and heavy leader it will not swim or drift well when it is fished. If a heavy fly is attached to a very light leader tippet its weight can snap it during the casting. Changing from light to heavy flies or vice versa means adding or taking off leader tippets. This calls for knots and a supply of leader tippett material.

Marking Your Line

It is a good idea to mark your lines. Suppose you have two or three lines and they're all the same color. You've put them away for the winter and, in the spring, you want the #7 and not the #6. How do you tell them apart? You can take a micrometer and check to see which is the larger of the two in diameter. That will be the #7. Or, if you were smart you would have put six little dots on the #6 line near its forward end and 7 dots on the #7.

Markings along your fly line's length can have a great value, too. For many years I've marked my fly lines with a single black marking about an inch long at the thirty-foot mark, two-inch-long bands, close together at forty feet, and a series of three black bands at fifty feet. If I'm waist deep in a good steelhead river, covering a fine run of water with few distinguishing marks like rocks or constant swirls of water in it, and I raise and miss a good fish, the first thing I'll do is to look at my line. There I'll see that one of the marks is two feet out of the tip top or another is halfway between the reel and the first guide. Knowing that, I can repeat the identical cast. I used to watch some of my customers at the fishing camp raise a good fish and then, perhaps because they felt that such a good fish should be farther away or demand more of them, like a longer cast, they'd strip off a yard or two of line before casting to the fish again. That would put the fly well beyond where the fish that rose wanted it—and they'd cast fruitlessly. If I called to them suggesting that they try a six-foot-shorter cast, they'd often hook the fish.

Knowing the exact distance of the cast that brought the fish up and showed his interest and then marking on the skyline the exact direction of the cast, I could lengthen or shorten my line and cast in any direction I chose to work on other fish; this way I could rest the one that rose and missed the fly. When I was ready to try again, I'd go back to the identical cast that raised him before. Then, if it got to be near lunchtime, I could look down at my feet to find some distinctive stone on the bottom and take references on the shores on two lines that crossed where I was standing and go in for soup and hash. When I came back I could find my casting spot and make other casts exactly like the one that first showed me where the fish was.

There's another mark you might want to put on your line. Those who use forward-tapered lines know that they should pick them up for the best back cast at a certain point, the point that will give them the full load of the forward section. A mark can tell them—perhaps of a different size or color than the thirty, forty, and fifty-foot marks which, when at the tip of the rod can mark the perfect pickup point. This pickup mark is only important when your casts will be in the medium to long range. Short casts can be picked up at any point short of the back taper for efficient short casting.

Knots

You'll need to know a few knots. There are dozens to choose from. You should choose knots that are simple to tie, so simple that you can practically tie them in the dark. First we need a knot to tie the fly to the leader. Joan's Clinch is quick and secure.

In order to get turned-up or turned-down eyed hooks to follow exactly the path of the leader it's tied to, use a turle knot; this is more trouble to tie, but you may feel that small difference is worth it. The turle can make your wet flies and streamers swim better but doesn't make a bit of difference with a dry fly, eye up or down or centered.

JOAN'S CLINCH

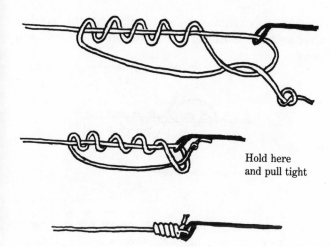

Hold here
and pull tight

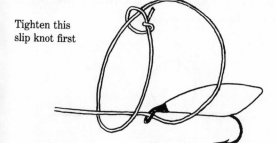

TURLE KNOT

Tighten this
slip knot first

Then tighten
loop behind eye

For tying monofilament to monofilament, the blood or barrel knot is traditional and professional. It's neat and strong.

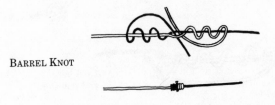

BARREL KNOT

When you need a simpler knot because your fingers are numb or it is getting dark, the surgeon's knot is a good one. One end of the two pieces of mono being joined must be free so that that end can be pulled twice through the knot loop as it is made. It's as strong as the barrel knot but not quite as neat looking.

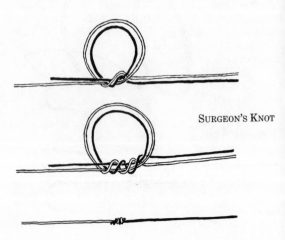

SURGEON'S KNOT

You'll need a knot to tie line to leader. The nail knot is the one I use. It holds like grim death when it is tied properly and slides through the guides well. A drop of Pliobond or other contact cement on the knot after it is tied can cover up any rough edges.

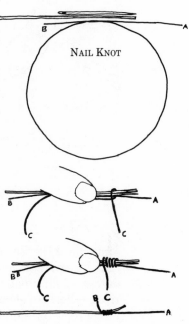

NAIL KNOT

Make loop, with leader end (A) and fly line (B). Lay needle and forward end of fly line on top, where mono overlaps and hold all materials firmly at that point.

Wind right-hand side of loop (C) around all three ends.

Wind five or six turns back *over* the section of leader loop you are winding with.

Grip windings, needle, line, and leader firmly and hold while you pull leader section (A) until all of loop is pulled through loops of mono.

Hold knot and back needle out; then pull gently at each end of monofilament to tighten wraps on fly line. Clip all ends and seal with drop of contact cement or epoxy.

For fly line to backing, an Albright knot is strong and simple.

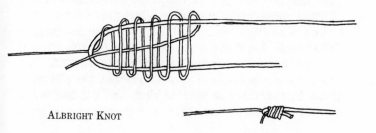

ALBRIGHT KNOT

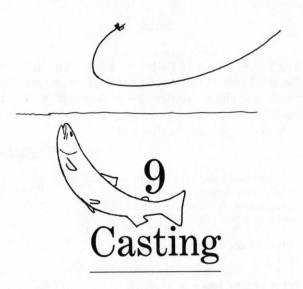

9
Casting

To project the almost weightless fly to where a fish may take it requires some skill at fly casting. Since there are dozens of different situations on a trout stream and a trout fisherman should be prepared to meet them all, a broad repertoire of fly-casting skills is essential.

The Roll Cast

The first cast to learn and one of the best is the roll cast. This is a one-stroke motion in which there is no correlation of multiple strokes. It has two main advantages. The first is that it can be made without any requirement of space behind the caster, something conventional overhead casting demands. The second is that it can be made even though the line may be slack and not laid out in front in a straight line. That is, roll casts can be made with slack line lying on the water in front or beside you—although, unless the line is on the surface, it may take two or more rolls to straighten the line out fully. This cast is generally used for shorter distances but long casts can be made with the right tackle. (In England, a caster named Grant roll cast for a hundred and twenty-seven feet.)

To roll cast, the line extending from the tip of the rod must have reasonable weight. The rod's forward motion puts energy into that section of the line and it carries right on down through the extended line to the end, lifting it from the water and rolling it out in a straight line. The drag of the water on the line before it is lifted in the "roll" is a requirement to make long casts. On grass, where the line slides freely, it is difficult to roll cast.

The best line for roll casting is a single or a "Triangle" taper in which the line increases in diameter continuously from the forward end of the line to the tip of the rod. Then, in the roll, heavy line is continually turning over lighter line which is more efficient than if the line must turn over line of its own weight. In that case, the energy is dissipated sooner and will not carry the cast as far.

1. To make a roll cast the rod should be held in an essentially vertical position with the line to be cast lying on the water in front of the caster. The hand should be above eye level and the elbow forward in the direction of the cast to be made. The high position gives a larger circle or loop and the height allows gravity to help a little more. The stroke will be made in the plane in which both shoulder and elbow are placed. The drive will be mainly with the forearm rather than the wrist.

2. Tilt the tip of the rod a little to the right, if you're a right-hander, so that the line will hang free and not tangle with the rod when you make the forward stroke.

3. The rod should come to a position angled back slightly so that the line hangs down at approximately the caster's shoulder. If the rod is angled forward the stroke length

THE ROLL CAST

Starting position

Roll forming

Line rolling out

will be diminished and the cast shortened. If it is angled back farther, it will throw the cast too high.

4. The line should come to a dead stop and hang directly downward at the tip of the rod. There is a tendency to hurry roll casts instead of lifting the rod slowly in preparation for the next cast. It is essential to wait until the line hangs even with or just behind the angler to make good roll casts.

When all four points have been taken care of, the cast is made by a quick forward and downward motion of the rod. This sends the line forward from the rod tip with enough force to form a circular loop that rolls out on the water, straightening out the line. The power of the cast must be matched to the length of line to be straightened out. The direction of the forward movement of the rod must not only be aimed in the target direction but adjusted as to how much forward and how much down. If the line lifts up and straightens out in the air (unless the caster wants it that way) there is too much "forward" and not enough "down" to make a good loop. If the stroke is aimed too low, the line will come down hard on the water and, again, will not make a good rolling loop.

As in all fly casting, the caster is at the mercy of the wind. If a wind is blowing toward a right-handed caster from his right, it can blow the line into his rod when the cast is made, causing a tangle. With such a wind the caster should change the rod to his left side for a backhand cast or cast with the other hand. Then the wind will blow the line away from rod and caster.

The roll cast can be made to a right-handed caster's left or to a left-hander's right or in the straight-ahead area. Otherwise, the line will cross itself in unrolling and the cast will fall apart. Remember not to cast *across* the line that is lying out on the water.

Overhead Casting

Overhead fly casting is unique among sports' strokes in that it requires as much force backward as forward. Instead of drifting back to the best position for a forward stroke which, when it is made, finishes the effort, fly casting's strokes range from two to many, all in a connected and synchronous sequence. Fly casting requires timing not only *within* the stroke but *between* the strokes. It is somewhat complicated but when done correctly it is not only efficient but beautiful.

If someone tells you fly casting is easy, ask them "Easier than what?"

It is certainly not easier than spinning or bait casting.

Fly line is not cast from the reel as in spinning and bait casting. It must be pulled from the reel by hand and then slid out through the guides by the process of casting. Line to the distance to be cast should be pulled from the reel by the left hand, which is the "line" hand (assuming you're a right-hander). The rod should be held in a pointed-down position, sloping downward at at least a 30° angle from the hand that holds the rod. Switching the rod back and forth in small, sharp movements as the line is being pulled from the reel will cause the line to flow through the guides and pile up on the water or grass in front of you. Lifting the rod to the roll-cast position and making a roll cast will straighten the line out in front of you, ready for casting of either style.

Typical fly casting has a back stroke and a forward stroke. The back stroke is designed to straighten out the line, in the air, in a direction as nearly opposite as possible from the direction in which the fly is to be cast. Having done that, at the precisely perfect time, the rod is moved forward, "loading" it to a good bend and adding a "power punch" when the *face of the rod* is perpendicular to the direction the fly is to be cast—just as a bat is perpendicular to the direction the ball it strikes will go. There must be enough power in the stroke to straighten out the

Lift off the water

Backcast unrolling

Forward cast power punch

line to the target. Too little power and the line will not fully straighten, too much and the line will straighten out and bounce back or land on the water with a fish-frightening splash.

That is the first and simplest exercise in fly casting. It is called "picking up and laying down." How accurately and smoothly it is accomplished will depend upon the physical pattern of the caster, on which muscles he uses and what arm movement. The arm hinges at three points—the wrist, the elbow, and the shoulder. All of them should be used in a balanced proportion. If only the wrist is used, the rod can only be moved in a circular swing pivoted on the wrist. Power, then, must come off on a tangent at a particular point that is difficult to determine. If we limit the wrist's pivoting and *move* it in the direction we want the fly line to go, we increase the power greatly.

Wrist action must be very limited. The tendency of a wrist caster is to put more motion in the wrist to gain more power. That motion simply carries the rod *beyond* the perfect point for the tangent, throwing the line down lower either in front or in back. Power, if it is to be effective, must be delivered before the tangential point is reached, meaning more power in the same short space of time there wasn't enough power delivered in before. Believe me, it is difficult to build up great speed and power in the allowable instant of time with wrist alone. A few people have done it but it takes time, practice, and the development of great wrist strength.

In fly casting the forearm and the forearm muscles are the most important. They can move to give a directional push to the rod and can swing it through the short power arc essential to good fly casting. The whole arm can swing from the shoulder. This makes lifting easier. A lifting back-cast swing tends to send the line higher in the air behind the caster so that, for medium distances, on the forward cast it is going *downhill* and the force of gravity will be helping on the cast instead of working against it.

There is an old saying, "A forward cast cannot be much better than the back cast that preceded it." Remember to keep your rod arm movement in one plane as you would in a good hammer stroke. To swing it out to the side puts your muscles at a disadvantage. Wrist, elbow, and shoulder should all work in the same plane.

I learned something about strokes the first time I saw a slow-motion film. It was back in 1925 in the first of the Grantland Rice "Sportlights" and showed Bobby Jones golfing. When I watched his drive in normal motion it looked like a continuous, smooth, and easy swing. When the same stroke was seen in slow motion I saw that just as Jones's club was about to hit the ball his muscles tensed, his face was tight, and I realized that all the effort he could put into his swing was going into it *at that moment*. Everything else was a matter of timing and bringing the club with the right speed and the right position for that final effort. So it is in casting. Putting hard effort into the whole stroke is tiring—and inefficient. Putting it in sharply only at the power punches makes for better, less-tiring fly casting.

Now we're ready to pick up and lay down. We have thirty-five feet of line and leader stretched out from the reel to the ground or water in front of us. The rod is pointed directly toward the bit of yarn or hookless fly we've attached to the end of the leader. (While practice can be done on either grass or water practice on water is better. The friction of the line going through the water is greater than over grass and it will, because of this increased resistance, "load" or bend the rod faster and more heavily.) We will be putting load into the rod like a charge in a battery and then, when, at the end of the back stroke we stop it, we count on that "charge" or energy to drive the fly line out behind us.

Watch the line on the water as you move the rod upward from the position where it points at your fly. You will lift swiftly with constantly *increasing* speed. As you see the leader about to leave the water, you should reach top speed, adding a slight wrist flip to the speed of your arm. That is the moment of the power punch, which, once delivered, ends the cast. That is the moment at which your rod's face should be aiming your line in the direction you want it to go. That direction is up and back and it should be determined by the angle of the line from rod tip to the point where it is leaving the water.

If you've had the right amount of power and applied it in the right direction, your line will straighten out at an upward angle behind you. You'll just wait for a bunch of milliseconds until it has straightened fully and then will make a forward cast to do the same thing. It will start and continue to accelerate to top speed. Then you will add a quick snap of your wrist, which will come at the moment the face of your rod is perpendicular to the line from there to the target. At that point you'll stop your rod motion and let it swing onward, releasing the power you've just put into it and sending the fly to the point of aim.

Now how easy does fly casting sound!

It isn't easy but it is a thing of power, grace, and beauty—and it's something you'll be proud and pleased to understand and do well.

Many fly casters in making their back-cast stroke move the rod butt in a convex arc. If they continue this arc beyond the point where the line leaves the water on the pick-up they will be throwing their back cast *down* behind them. This is out of their vision and they are surprised and disappointed when the following forward cast drives up into the air instead of out toward the target because it wants to go 180° from where the back cast started. A way to correct this low back-cast fault is to make the back-cast arm stroke concave instead of convex. Then if the concave arc is continued beyond the normal point for ending the stroke the back cast will be thrown *higher* instead of lower and the forward cast can still be made directly to the target. This concave motion with a power

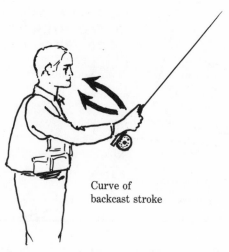

Curve of
backcast stroke

punch that curves upward is a part of what I call the oval
casting technique. This draws the line in low and lifts it
for the back cast but whether in oval or conventional
casting this concave motion will prevent the back cast
from falling too low. To make the cast movement concave,
the caster should make sure his hand moves back on the
stroke before it moves upward.

One of the most common faults in picking the line up
from the water for another cast is to hold the rod too
high. We call this the "still fisherman's syndrome." Most
pictures of anglers usually show them with rod at a high
angle and the line hanging down limply from the tip, as
if waiting for a nibble and a float to go down. That high
angle between rod and line is said to have been the origin
of the name "angler." The trouble with that position is
that the backward arc for the back cast is limited, usually
to a point where not enough power can be put into the
cast to straighten it out.

The rod should *start from a very low position*, pointed
directly at the fly. That gives a full swing before the near-
vertical point for the back cast is reached. Every degree
the rod is lifted before the cast is started is a degree lost.

POWER SNAP ENDING BACK CAST
MUST STOP AT THIS VERTICAL LINE

THIS ANGLE TOO
SMALL FOR
BACK CAST

STILL FISHERMAN'S SYNDROME
ROD TOO HIGH TO MAKE
A GOOD BACK CAST

CORRECT
ROD POSITION
THIS LOW ANGLE
BEST FOR
GOOD BACK CAST

A

B

A1

LOWERING ROD FROM A DOES NOT HELP
THIS SLACK WILL
PREVENT LOADING →
AND SPOIL CAST

When starting with the rod high in front of you, it is quite natural, in order to put in enough power to make the cast, to carry it well back beyond the vertical, driving the line down low behind the caster and to a very poor position for a good forward cast.

I was over forty before I decided to make every cast a good one. I talked to myself quite a bit and every time I found my rod higher than it should have been for a good back cast I did a penance. Either I lowered my rod and stepped back a few paces to take out the slack and bring the rod tight to the line or I made a roll cast and held my rod down low to the water at the end of it. Eventually it became a habit. You ought to make it your habit, too.

The roll pick-up is a valuable adjunct to normal casting. It helps out when there's slack in the line that would make it difficult to pick up—as in the case where a caster has assumed the "still-fisherman" position. By lifting the rod on up to a roll-cast position (remember the four requirements) and making a roll cast, the line will straighten out on or above the water far enough to give a good loading of the rod when a back cast is made. In the roll-cast, lift the line completely off the water; this will give you an even better back cast in a shorter time.

Correcting and Perfecting

Here are some of the things that can happen in fly casting and what causes them.

If you hear a loud snap when you start the forward cast, it is either because you started your forward cast too soon or you didn't have enough power in your back cast to straighten out your line. The main reason for starting the forward cast too soon is because you've been thinking that fly casting is a thing of fast action. It is. But there are pauses between the action that must be precisely timed. Remember that the line must straighten out fully on the back cast in order to make a good forward cast to the water.

Lack of power in the back cast is a hangover from all the other sport strokes you've been making all your life. You drifted back easily and then whacked the hell out of it forward. That's what you tried to do with your fly rod and it didn't work. Equal power either way. It is instinctive to try to make up with our forward-throwing muscles what we lack in backward-throwing muscles. Recognize the need and put a greater effort, proportionately, into your back cast than your fore cast. Make them balance.

Suppose your line went high in the air in front of you and then fell in a heap instead of straightening out to the target. That is because you didn't keep your back cast high. You may have tried to put a little extra energy into your back cast and put it in *after* your rod was aimed at the proper slightly upward back-cast position. Your extra effort carried the rod too far back in its arc and you aimed your back cast *down* behind you. From that low position the forward drive takes your line out on too high an angle. A watcher can tell you what you're doing wrong and then you can correct it. Or, as we'll cover later on, you can cast horizontally so that you can watch your rod and line during the entire cast and *see* your mistakes.

Suppose, on the other hand, your line splashed down on the water close in front of you. That will happen when you've continued your forward swing too long and put in forward power downward after you've reached the proper aim point and should have stopped. Your rod will be in your vision in front of you and if you make that mistake, you should be able to see and avoid it.

A friend can tell you when your wrist is breaking back too far and bringing your back cast too low—or tell you of another fault that some casters do instinctively. They make a good back stroke and then, instead of leaving their arm back, or even drifting it back even more to get a longer forward stroke, they drift their arm forward while waiting for the line to straighten out behind them. This cuts down the length of the forward stroke, limiting the power they can put into it and limiting the length of the cast.

Actually, a caster can see a good deal of what is going on. He can see the position of his hand and of the rod butt in it. The rod butt controls the rod's action and is the key to casting. As you move the butt, so moves the rod. The forward unrolling of the cast is in full view and the time it takes for the forward cast is the time required for a back cast of equal length. But to see it all, one should cast in a horizontal plane centered in front so that, by swinging his head as if at a tennis match, the entire cast is visible.

A video camera can help. Just as tape recorders helped people develop good speaking abilities (without a recorder no one ever hears his own voice as it sounds to others) the video will show you the casting faults you cannot see.

Casting horizontally can help, too. Your reel should be horizontal and your thumb (or forefinger) pressed against the rod grip on the opposite side. The reel should always come off the grip in the direction you want to cast. Roll cast your line out straight. Now make a back cast and let it fall to the grass. (This type of practice should be done on grass.) See where it landed. It should fall at a point 90° to the right of your rod tip as you stand for the casting. If it doesn't, change it to that position. Then make your forward cast to straighten out the line 180° from where it lies; that's in exactly the opposite direction. As you practice to move the line from one side to the other to end up in these opposite directions, you'll recognize the angle of the stroke required. If the angle is too large, you'll bend the line around behind you. If it's too small, you'll have it stretch out in front of the point you're aiming at. Practice until your muscles accustom to the stroke you need. Then, instead of allowing the line to fall to the grass at the end of each stroke, keep it in the air and false cast with the line still straightening out, back and forth, in opposite directions. Your final step is to lift your rod up and cast, in the *same manner*, overhead, forward, and back.

This casting without delivering the fly is called "false casting" and it is an important part of fly casting. If a little extra power is put into one or both of the directional casts a little line (which you have already pulled from the reel) can be slid out through the guides to make the line you are casting in the air that much longer. That's called "shooting line" and it is the method by which line is lengthened during the casting period.

By now you have realized that there is a time period required for the line to straighten out on each cast. That period, called "drift time," can be put to good use. Let's say you want to make a low cast under a bush. That means you'll want your back cast to be low so that a forward cast exactly 180° from the line will also be low and go under the bush. During the drift time on the back cast you can let your rod tip drop to the side at the same speed and to the same level your straightened-out back cast is falling; and make your forward cast from that new low level. Drift time will let you reposition your rod for a forward cast in a new direction but it can do more than that. It can give you the key to perfect timing.

Everyone has waved a banner and managed to wave it smoothly so that it does not sag and bounce. To do that, constant pressure must be maintained on the pennant lest it droop. During the drift time, a fly caster can maintain constant pressure on his line from the rod. Not enough pressure to move it—just enough to know where it is and what it is doing. This will let you swing a back cast a little to one side and realize that it is going there. It will let you feel that the rod is swinging a little farther to one side to reach the right point to make the forward swing at a different angle to a different point in the river. Constant pressure will give you a oneness with your tackle, make it more a part of you.

Timing could be figured out by calculations on a computer. Suppose you are false casting thirty-five feet of line and leader back and forth. You descide to let out another three feet. How many more milliseconds do you wait on the back cast before starting forward. If you do figure it out, and I think it would take a lot of knowledge and time to manage it, and the answer comes out, say, 7 milliseconds, you then must know just how long that time period is and, as you wait for your back cast to straighten out, add it to the rest of the dead time you've been leaving between the previous casts. It doesn't sound simple and it isn't. In a case like this your muscles can "think" faster than your brain. Think of your line as a banner and wave (cast) it smoothly.

You've heard the old saying that "You can't catch fish unless your fly is in the water." It's worth remembering. To do that one should make his line pickups at that right spot and make the forward cast after a single back cast if he can. False casts take time; and most of them, made beyond the right pickup points when making longer casts, cause trouble rather than making the longer casts easier. Once you have that forward belly out of the rod tip you should be able to cast just about as far as if you had extended more line out of the guides. The more line you extend beyond that point the more critical your timing becomes and the harder it is to determine the right time for full power on the delivery cast.

When I started using short, light rods for big salmon I had to bring my engineering education back into play. As a graduate civil engineer I knew that the formula for kinetic energy, the energy of motion, is $\frac{1}{2}MV^2$. Translated, that means half the mass (weight) multiplied by the square of the velocity.

The formula makes it obvious that if you double the weight of the line you're moving you double the energy. Just as obvious is that if you double the velocity at which you move the same line you quadruple the energy. I decided that *speed* was the answer when I started using shorter and shorter rods.

To gain greater speed I had to lengthen my stroke just as if I were throwing a javelin or throwing a ball. Little rods are usually built for small people to fish in small streams where they don't have to cast very far. I needed a little extra power just above the grip so that the rod would show life and not drag when I pushed it forward at full power. Except for that small extra stiffness there, my rods were very delicate. They were of split bamboo and weighed less than an ounce and three quarters. The very light lines used on most short, light rods are not heavy enough to drive through the air resistance and are at the mercy of the wind. I continued to use the same weight line I was using, approximately a #7, and balanced the shorter rods to it.

Another factor of importance I knew because I was a pilot. Add three inches to a six-foot-long propeller and you'll reduce the revolutions per minute the motor will turn it at by at least three hundred. Air pressure against our bodies is fifteen pounds per square inch at sea level. Pushing a long rod through the air takes more effort than pushing a short one. I ran tests and found I could get 25 percent more speed at the fly using a six-foot rod than I could with one that was nine feet long. Playing a fish was no problem. As anyone knows who has ever played a marlin on light gear—like a two-hundred pounder on a 30-pound-test line—knows it is not the ability to pull the fish around through the water that tires him but the effort he puts into his runs and leaps to escape. A trout's own efforts will tire him out.

Because the rods were short it was hard to keep my back cast high enough to get good distance. In order to do so, I broke with conventional casting. In conventional casting the fly moves through a figure-of-eight path. It goes out forward, dropping, swings around and climbs on the back cast until it drops and swings again to come forward finally on a path similar to the first cast.

I put my fly into an *oval of travel* in which it never crossed its own path. I reasoned that if I got my line as low as possible as it came past me on the back cast and lifted it up on the back stroke it would be higher at the end of the back cast. Meanwhile, I'd be reaching my right (rod) hand back as far and as high as I could and it would be poised there for the longest possible forward stroke, using the muscles I'd use in throwing a ball as hard and as fast as I could. A baseball pitcher can make his hand move at almost a hundred miles an hour. I'm sure I could make mine move at at least seventy-five. Add to that seventy-five-mile speed the flip forward of the line by the rod and it is easy to see that I could develop the speed required for a long cast.

The oval is not a perfect one. It will twist a little in the wind and vary according to side pressures—but it flows smoothly. It is like the waving of a banner at varying speeds through a full backward and forward cycle. It can be a lazy form of casting and during false casting the speed of the line can be increased or diminished at will.

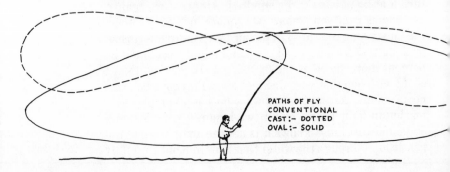

PATHS OF FLY
CONVENTIONAL
CAST :- DOTTED
OVAL :- SOLID

When the line is in the right position for the forward delivery cast, all possible power can be applied, knowing that the line is putting the necessary load on the rod to utilize its capabilities. Casts can be made in the conventional overhead plane or to the side. The oval gives a wide range of casting options.

One of those is to vary the length of the back cast. There is a certain amount of "roll" in my casting. I send a section of line forward with enough speed and power to make the trailing line follow it as a roll cast follows the movement of the line at the rod tip. So if I want to shorten the length of a back cast while still casting the same length of line I start forward a little sooner, putting a little extra "roll" into the forward cast with a slightly longer power punch. I save the time required for a full back cast which over a full fishing day will have my fly in the water many more minutes. I do this commonly with such heavier flies as streamers because the slightly wider loop I send forward will be less likely to let the fly tangle with the line as it unrolls in a wind.

Reduced backcast—
oval casting

I can vary this length of back cast to a minimum, which I call an "air roll." In this cast I bring in the line as low as possible beside me and, as soon as I have a couple of feet behind the rod tip, I make a very swift and powerful roll cast. Timing is critical. But with this cast you can lift your line from the water on the retrieve and roll it out again for forty feet or so with less than a ten-foot space behind you. Because the fly comes in swiftly *through the air*, this cast works well for dry flies, which could not be dried off in a simple roll cast. It will let me change direction easily between pickup and forward cast. This cast and the rest of oval casting makes up much of my fly fishing.

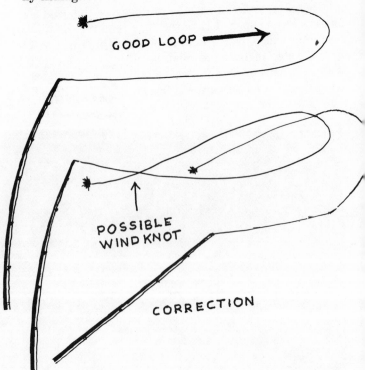

GOOD LOOP

POSSIBLE WIND KNOT

CORRECTION

when the line has loaded the rod for the next stroke, even though line may be extended during the cast. A longer line in the air calls for a slightly longer stroke and a longer waiting period for the line to straighten out. How much longer? Determining just how many more milliseconds must be allowed for perfect timing if three feet is added at your particular casting speed would be a complicated job for a mathematician with a computer, but my muscles will tell me instantly as I "feel" the line's changing pressures.

Any weight at the end of a fly line is a casting burden. It takes a fairly heavy line to control a heavy fly although any fly line will cast a light one. *Any* weight other than the line tends to conflict with casting. If the back cast is not perfect and the caster starts the line moving forward while a heavy fly is still moving backward, there'll be trouble. Each of the masses, the line and the fly, have their own $\frac{1}{2}MV^2$ of energy and they're going in opposite directions. Usually the line will overpower the fly. The fly will come to a jerking halt, then snap back in the line's direction faster than the line is traveling, causing a tangle.

When you're casting a weighted fly, make sure your line and fly are *straightened out completely* on the back cast before you make a forward cast. If the fly is not too heavy, it is possible to straighten out both back casts and forward casts and even shoot a little line in the process but that is for the experts only. When fishing weighted nymphs, slow casts that straighten out in both directions are a must. Long rods help and being tall helps, too. Cast as softly and as smoothly as possible whenever heavy or weighted flies are being cast.

The Double Haul

The double haul is a technique of casting by which we can increase distance and gain more control. Hauling on the line moves it through the guides; when added to a normal casting stroke, this gives additional speed to the line.

Just at the turnover point, the line is moving forward as fast as the rod alone can make it go. The line pull of the haul makes the whole line move just that much faster. As we mentioned, $\frac{1}{2}MV^2$ applies and the energy of the line is increased at the square rate. It is an adding of power by the left (line) hand to whatever the right hand contributes. When the double haul came into play, tournament casting distances jumped some forty feet.

The movement of both hands must be coordinated precisely for the hauls to work. There is an easy way to develop that coordination. Get out on the meadow again and set up to cast horizontally. Use about thirty or thirty-five feet of line. You'll be casting it to points 180° apart on a line through the tip of your rod. You'll make the cast and let the line land, straightened out, on each side.

Set yourself with a tree or some conspicuous object

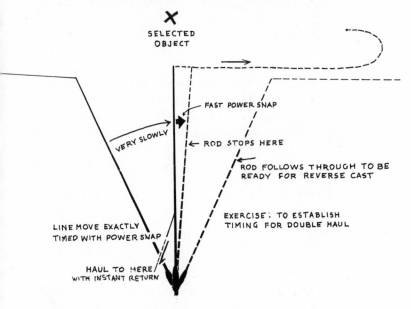

X
SELECTED
OBJECT

FAST POWER SNAP

VERY SLOWLY

← ROD STOPS HERE

ROD FOLLOWS THROUGH TO BE
READY FOR REVERSE CAST

LINE MOVE EXACTLY
TIMED WITH POWER SNAP

EXERCISE: TO ESTABLISH
TIMING FOR DOUBLE HAUL

HAUL TO HERE
WITH INSTANT RETURN

the tail end of a squall help me straighten out my back cast and then drive my forward cast into a relatively quiet time in the wind. That made the difference between having almost all my casts wind-broken and making fewer casts but good ones. Wind is only smooth over large stretches of water or level land. Since most of the streams we fish are in uneven land, we have a chance to make the gusts and quiet spots help in our casting.

It takes strength and speed to cast into a strong wind. Once, in Iceland, where winds can really blow, Joan and I were faced with gale winds behind us. I was almost, but not quite, able to reach a lie where I'd seen a fish roll. I didn't have enough power to get any sort of a back cast. As has been mentioned we have more strength throwing forward than to the rear. By turning to face the wind on our back casts we were able to drive back casts into it for a greater distance and, spinning around in a quick motion, the forward casts, *with* the wind, went out the extra ten feet needed and we could reach the fish.

(Turning to make a back cast can be valuable, too, when it is necessary to put it into a hole in the bushes or between some trees. In that way you can see where your back cast is going. Turning for the forward cast, you can then direct it to the perfect spot.)

An ice boat can sail *faster* than the wind that drives it by sailing at an angle. A fly caster can find ways to let the wind help him by getting his line into a position where the wind will carry it in the direction he wants it to go. Windy days are often good for fishing. The surface is roughened; leaders will not be as conspicuous; a splashing fly will not be as frightening. There's even less competition from other anglers. There are many advantages to fishing on windy days—not least of which is that the wind often carries food, such as grasshoppers, and fish may be more likely to forage then. Learning to cast in the wind can help you avoid missing many good fishing hours.

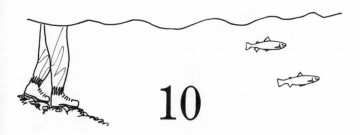

10

Approach and Presentation

No aspects of fly fishing require more of the predator's temperament than approach and presentation.

Knowing where the trout lie, how do you approach them? How do you present your fly?

I believe dedicated youngsters do it best. I can remember crawling carefully to the stream banks through the alders and reaching the pool without alarming the fish. Then I watched them and, finally, I poked a pole carefully through the branches to let a worm drop lightly to the water in front of a trout. If I made a false move and frightened the fish, I'd often wait quietly until the trout assumed all danger was past and came out to his feeding station again. This is stalking at its most interesting level.

most fishermen on most waters feel the need for waist or chest waders that give them the option of keeping dry and wading deep.

Back in the thirties when waders were first coming into general use, there were stories going the rounds of how trout fishermen, wearing them, were found drifting around in the eddies of trout streams with their wader feet up (because of the air trapped in them) and their poor heads under water, drowned dead.

To find out the truth, I went to Buffum's Corner on the Battenkill and jumped from the bridge so that a photographer could get a picture of me halfway down the twenty-foot drop, head down, air trapped in my waders without a belt, diving into the pool below. I made two mistakes. It was fall when I got the idea and the water was down in the forties and cold; also, I wore a sweater and the knitted sleeves soaked up water like a sponge, making it difficult to lift my arms out of the water in a crawl stroke. But I swam around side stroke without any trouble and soon came ashore.

Then, to avoid trapping any air in the waders, I waded in slowly, to expel it all—and I then swam around again. As I expected, it was a little more difficult to swim *without* any air trapped in the waders than it was *with* trapped air. The human body floats because of the air in our lungs. Expel all the air and it will sink. Air trapped in waders is an advantage rather than a hazard. I have known anglers wearing boots or waders to fall in and drown—but I am sure this was caused by panic rather than the waders.

Some fishermen wear belts around their waders. They do look trimmer that way. Anglers have told me that then, if they splash water over the tops, it will stop at the belt; I don't believe this. I don't wear a belt because I find that walking in waders is very often warm work and that any air circulation I can get into my wader legs will let me be cooler. Belt or no belt is a wader's personal preference, not a matter of safety.

A wader should be prudent and careful. But if he does go in over his waders or falls in while wearing them he shouldn't be in any danger. If he can't swim and simply does a dead man's float, taking deep breaths periodically and letting his face sink into the water between breaths, he'll stay afloat and should drift to shallower water. If not, he can do a dog paddle between his breaths and make his way to the shore. If doing that frightens a wader, he should avoid getting near deep water. However, if he can get to shore without waders, he should be able to get to shore *with* them, especially if he's trapped enough air in them to make up for the small extra weight of waders or shoes. Since water is fairly heavy ("A pint's a pound the world around") waders don't weigh much under water and therefore aren't too hard to swim with or in.

If you do have any fears about wading dangers, go down to the stream some warm summer afternoon; take anything you don't want to get wet out of your vest and pockets, and then fall in on purpose. Take a friend along just to feel safe if you need one or take a long rope and tie it to a tree on shore.

The worst thing about falling in is damage to your ego. When anyone falls in, the first thing they do is to take a quick look around to see who saw them. But it's a rare fisherman who doesn't fall in or lose a fish once in a while. The occasional dunking is a small price to pay for the pleasures and extra fish wading will give you. The ability to reach a few difficult fish makes the difference, often, between an ordinary day and a very good one.

Wading staffs can give stability where currents are swift and greater security where streambeds are rough. They're a nuisance if they have to be carried, full length, because they drag in the water and they can trip you or tangle your line. If you need the additional security, they're worth it—but there are folding wading staffs now available that can be carried out of the way in a holster or a vest and extended when necessary to get through a bad stretch of water.

in which there is always something to learn, some puzzle to be solved.

So the wet-fly fisherman, in full view of the trout at his casting distance, moves directly downstream toward him. He catches trout because his person, at that distance, is not deemed a threat and because the trout does not connect the angler's fly with the angler. His mind cannot conceive such things as line and leader. With the angler at a safe distance, he feels free to feed. If he is suspicious, it will be because the fly may not move correctly or a part of the leader at the fly will make it look unnatural. Then, too, he may not be hungry or may not think he'll like the taste of what he sees.

Having fished for that trout and failed to catch him, the angler moves on and fishes for the others still to come, giving up on that one which will soon be so close he will be alarmed and would not take a fly. There is a certain distance an angler should cast his wet fly. A lesser distance will bring him too close to the trout he is fishing for.

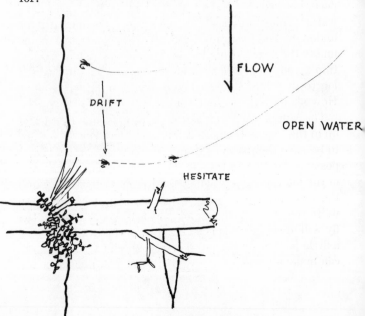

The wet-fly fisherman will cover the water best if he extends his casting range by a uniform distance, each time. If, as he starts casting, he lengthens his cast by about a yard each time until he reaches the casting distance he wishes to maintain down through the run, and then takes a single step between each cast, he will have his fly pass within eighteen inches, vertically, of every fish within his casting range. Uniform coverage leaves no blank spots where the biggest fish in the pool might escape having the fly come within striking range.

The spread between casts may be any distance the angler chooses. A six-foot distance will let you cover the pool in half the time. A two-foot spread will make your fishing more intensive. The uniform coverage is for use when you do not know particular places where fish are most likely to lie. If you know and recognize such hot spots, then it is wise to make several casts to each of them as you move along.

Open-water coverages with wet fly or streamer are simple. The presentation becomes more complex when you think you know where a particular fish is lying. Suppose there is a log end sticking out of the bank over deep water. You can guess that there'll be a good trout lying under it. You can guess, too, that his head will be just under the log and his tail extending out below it. You think, too, that he'll lie well out toward the end of the log to give him access to more of the deep water flow. How should you present your streamer?

The worst thing you can do is to get your fly caught up in the log itself where it touches the water. You want to be sure the fish sees it and that it is as convenient as possible for him to take it. If you cast right to the end of the log the current will move the fly away swiftly and the fish may not feel it's worth the long chase to catch it. If you cast above the log and retrieve normally, the fly will move past his nose at high speed. But if you cast a little farther upstream to give yourself extra time, you can make a normal retrieve to a point just above the log

Most anglers of that time fished with fairly long rods and since trout were more plentiful and unsophisticated they could be caught with fairly short lines. When eyed hooks came in and dry flies became the ruling favorites, matters changed. A single dry fly was fished because two or three on the same leader caused one of them to drag and look unnatural. Fishermen found that finer leaders were necessary to fool fish. Two or more flies on them tended to tangle. With the more sophisticated trout, catching more than one trout on a three-fly leader became quite rare. Most-wet-fly fishermen joined the dry-fly fishermen and switched from three flies to one. There are a few of us who still use dropper flies at least part of the time.

A dropper fly is put on a leader about eighteen to twenty-four inches from the tail fly. The extending leader section is made by leaving about five inches as an extending length when the tail tippet is tied on. The disadvantage is that a dropper fly will tangle, especially if the leader is fine. The advantage is that you're giving the trout a choice of two flies. If you find that the trout are consistently taking the dropper, it can be made the tail fly and the original tail fly eliminated. A nymph or wet fly as a dropper and a streamer at the tail makes a good combination. The larger streamer can be seen at a greater distance by the trout; though he may not want it, he'll see the wet fly, which he may want. Whatever the combination of flies, two are more conspicuous than one. Some anglers put the streamer ahead of a nymph, using a stronger leader up to the streamer and a very light one behind the streamer to give the trailing nymph or wet fly more action in the water and a less visible leader tippet to fool the trout better.

An excellent presentation, particularly in slower waters with sophisticated trout, is to let a weighted sculpin-like streamer settle to the bottom and rest there for a few seconds before giving it life. This has been so effective for me that I've designed a special weighted sculpin imitation with broad soft pectoral fins to ride with the hook upright and not snag as it sinks to or moves across the streambed.

be pulling his dry fly across the surface in an unnatural dragging retrieve right in front of all the fish he's moving down to fish. The swimming of the wet fly across in front of them may only stir their interest as they wait for it to reach them; the dragging dry fly can be counted on to put them off. This is conventional wisdom. There are no absolute truths in fishing and as soon as one says "always" or "never" he's in for a shock, for trout are as varied and inconsistent as we humans are. There is always the exception to break the rule. There are always times when the unconventional or absurd will catch fish that ignore all the tried and true methods.

I mentioned earlier that I usually give wet flies a movement I believe is fitting for their size. One day when several of us were fishing Cairns' Pool on the Beaverkill with little luck, a fisherman waded in and fished his wet fly by ripping it along a foot or two at a time on the retrieve. He caught a few fish in short order and left. Were the fish intrigued by his unnatural retrieve? Did they think he had a super bug, a speed swimmer they'd never seen before and, therefore, wanted to try? Not all fishing is reasonable.

The consensus is that free-floating flies are more natural and better, but dry flies *can* be dragged across the surface and fish will take them. Motion is the sign of life and sometimes it works with dry flies when a totally free drift will not—but this makes your leader movement far more conspicuous and is unlikely to work on still waters or with sophisticated trout. Fly fishermen are always torn between exact imitations and flies no trout would ever expect to see, between natural actions and wild or strange movements. Learn the rules first—but then, in order to be more effective, learn when to break them.

The dry-fly fisherman should move upstream as he fishes. This will help avoid dragging dry flies across the surface in the face of fish you have yet to fish for. But the dry-fly cast can be in any direction. Suppose you see a fish rise and it's a good one. You can look over the situation and decide that the best presentation you can make is from well above him. You leave your position and plan a presentation for that particular fish. Casting a dry fly from upstream of a fish has definite advantages. With a cast from above the fly comes to the fish before the leader and line. It drifts freely and is least likely to develop drag if it comes to him from that direction. An added advantage is that the angler can strip line from the reel and let it drift freely behind the line already on the water, something that cannot be done except from that upstream angle. You can make a long cast, standing far away from the fish and then strip off line to let your fly drift to a fish that is beyond your casting range. For the fish you know are good ones and important to you always consider a dry-fly cast from above.

The easiest dry-fly presentations are directly across the stream. Then one can make a cast to a point upstream of the fish, have it drift down over him, and pick it up for another cast to the same area without having to strip line either in or out. There is no need then for more than one back cast before the presentation cast is made, no lengthening and shortening of line. The ideal situation is for across-the-stream casts and an upstream progression. If the cast must be made at an upstream angle, the caster must strip in line as the fly drifts closer to both the fish and himself. Then he must false cast to extend it to the necessary distance to reach upstream again. The more upstream the cast the more work it is to make each presentation.

Dry-fly fishing is sometimes said to be low-water fishing or summer fishing. In truth, dry flies will work anytime the fish are warmed up enough to come to the surface for food. The difference between wet and dry-fly fishing is mainly in the amount of water covered. One can compare the water covered in four wet-fly casts and that covered with four dry-fly casts. The dry fly drifts slower

frightened by the unnatural action of the fly on the previous cast. On the other hand, allowing the fly to drift on through may well bring a strike. And subsequent casts can be made without alarming the fish. It's worthwhile to make a habit of picking dry flies up as gently as possible for the back cast. A fish that is frightened at one spot may run to another and fear in one fish engenders fear in the others that see or sense his motion. An entire run or pool can be ruined by such thoughtlessness.

It is always important to consider what is natural to a fish. In nature, straight lines are pretty rare. That's why telephone lines and railroad tracks, which are as straight as we can make them, are so conspicuous. They stand out like sore thumbs on a hillside or in a valley. Is it more natural to expect a grasshopper to be floating down the stream in the middle of some twisted straws than perched at the very end of a single straw? Is your fly more natural looking to a fish if it is at the end of a straight leader or if it is at the end of a curving piece of floating filament. Most of us have been surprised to have a good fish come up and take a dry fly after we've made a lousy cast and dropped it in the middle of a mess of twisted mono. Lots of things drift down on the stream's surface and bugs often drift along with them. Leaders for dry flies may be least likely to alarm a fish when they're *not* straight.

We worry about our leaders floating. There's no question but that a leader *on* the surface is more visible than one under it. We've all seen those big shadows on the streambed when the sun shines brightly on clear waters, shadows that vanish when the leader sinks. What can we do about it? The floating is caused by the surface tension of the water. In physics we learned that a steel needle will float on still water if it is placed on the surface gently. We have to break the surface tension with our leader to make it sink. That's not too difficult with the larger diameters but when we get down to diameters of .005 and .004 inches (6X and 7X) it becomes next to impossible.

In rippled water, it is easy to sink a leader because the surface motion breaks the surface tension. But we don't need fine tippets under rippled water conditions. It's when the air is still and warm and the water smooth that we have most leader problems. If we soak our leaders in a tension breaker like glycerine or soap, they'll sink readily, but when we cast them swiftly (a cast can move through the air at over a hundred miles an hour) to the fish sixty feet away, such coatings are soon stripped from the hard mono surface and we end up with tippets that float. Most of the time we have to live with floating tippets. I used to use sewing-thread tippets that, because they were braided or twisted, would absorb water rather than repel it as gut and nylon do. They sank well and were so soft that a floating fly would swing around in almost any eddy instead of being pulled *across* it unnaturally by the stiffer gut or nylon; but they tangled easily and twisted readily if the fly was the least bit off balance. I did catch some difficult fish with the thread leaders but decided, in the end, they weren't worth the trouble once very fine monofilament became available.

If, when the leader has settled to the water and the line and part of the butt of the leader have sunk, an angler pulls on the line, that motion will break the surface tension and sink the floating part of the leader. With gentle pulls the entire leader can be sunk until only the fly is floating at the end of a sunken, almost-invisible leader. To achieve this, one has to cast upstream and beyond the fish far enough so that the entire leader can be sunk and the fly pulled to exactly the right spot to present it to the fish. Some trout are worth that trouble and some anglers have the eyesight and gentle touch to accomplish such a maneuver.

Many other things may put the fish off. The dry fly may not be a good imitation but in that case the fish will rarely come up and look at it. When he does that, you know you're close. If it isn't the fineness of the leader

It is possible to "break through" a hatch by giving the trout something far different that they like as well or better. A streamer will sometimes take trout that are rising steadily to small insects. A drifted beetle or a grasshopper can be tempting for a momentary change. A stonefly nymph is always a pleasurable part of a trout's diet. Instead of *almost* matching a small or difficult insect, why not use one of your successful imitations of some other type of trout food, or challenge these with an attractor?

I spent one summer trying this: whenever I encountered a hatch, I first worked to match it and then, having accomplished it, tried to break through it with nymphs, streamers, and terrestrials. In almost every case, I was successful and took fish almost as readily on the non-hatchers as on the hatch imitations. Skunked we may be, but let's go down trying strange things, if necessary. Big trout, for instance, have a love for the mice or voles that occasionally fall into the stream. A mouse is a meal and a half and the chance to get that much good food in one gulp is not often passed up by a really hungry trout. Just because most of the insects trout take are relatively small, this doesn't mean that they won't take almost anything they can get into their mouths if they think it nourishing and tasty. Before using a mouse or a big streamer, though, be sure your leader is strong enough and that your imitation acts as a mouse or minnow should.

Having a dry fly float freely without drag can be difficult to manage. When there are conflicting currents in the floating area or when a fast current lies between the angler and the fly, drag will develop if a normal cast is used. The angler needs slack in the leader *at the fly*. Slack can be put into casts in several ways. Drawing back on the rod just as the line has straightened out will make the line fall like a snake, with slack all along its length. Since the only slack that is of any value has to be right at the fly, most of this slack has no value to the fisherman. Concentrate the slack at the fly.

This can be done best, I believe, by making what we call a "plop" cast. Cast with a wide loop and let the cast run out of power just as the loop is about to straighten out. Instead of straightening, the leader will simply plop down in a mess. It takes practice and precision to make this cast but it can give your dry fly a long float in swift and complicated currents. Because the leader is pulled away by the currents in the same order that its coils or twists fell, it will not tangle.

A long leader is an advantage here. Piling up a lot of falling leader is less likely to upset a trout than piling up a shorter leader and some of the bulkier fly line. Sometimes I'll use a thirty-foot leader, the last ten being 7X, and pile it up for very long floats in pocket water, using wide loops that never cause a wind knot or tangle. Learning to cast long leaders can be a great advantage. More and more of the trout we fish for are sophisticated—and longer and finer leaders will catch more of those fish when conditions are tough.

Another way to give slack at the fly is to make a cast that straightens out the line at a high upward angle. The line, being heavier, falls first and a long, fine leader following it down is drawn back to fall in a heap, giving slack for a long drift.

Nymphs

The trickiest of presentations is a free-drifting nymph. A nymph can be made to swim as a wet fly does and it can be quite effective. But it will be more effective than a wet fly since it is a more natural pattern to be underwater than most wet-fly patterns are. Most nymphs, however, do not swim as fast as a wet fly moves. Their swimming capabilities are limited and they often drift with the current more than they swim. Most of them are crawlers rather than swimmers. They've come from the streambed and not the surface. They should drift along

and leader and the front taper sink much more slowly at a fairly steep angle. In order to get the nymph down to the same level the belly of the line has sunk to, we have to draw it *in* for about fourteen feet. In essence, that means that we have to cast fourteen feet beyond the deep spot where we think the fish is. From there on in, though, we get a deep retrieve.

By shortening the leader and cutting off the finer end of the taper of the line, the distance to be cast can be shortened. Or some weight can be added on or near the nymph to take it down as fast as the belly of the line sinks. This takes us back to the problem of having to cast with a weight at the end of the leader.

Suppose you cast across the stream and the current is moving at three feet per second and sinking at a rate of half an inch per second. In being swept thirty feet downstream by the current, the line will sink only five inches. That's not a lot when you're fishing in four feet of water. But it tells us that sinking lines work better in still water than in streams and that the faster a river flows the less depth we can get on our casts. A concentrated weight, at the fly, will sink faster if the weight is heavy enough—and it need not be too heavy for most nymphs, if it sinks on a slack leader.

So we weight our nymph and sink it down to the trout's level and get it to drift along, just above the streambed. Remember, we've had to cast with some slack at the nymph so that it will sink without being held back by the

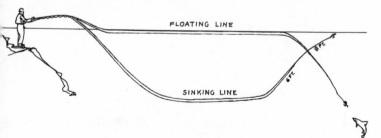

drag of the line. Suppose we manage that. We find that
our nymph, in order to carry the weight, has to be fairly
large. And we notice, too, that it has become a sort of
feathered sinker, which does not respond to the vagaries
of the current as a real, free-drifting nymph does. Or
suppose we decide to use a very small nymph on a #16
hook. There is no way we can put enough lead wire on a
#16 hook to get it to sink fast enough. We can solve both
those problems at one stroke. We use unweighted nymphs
and put our weight ahead of the nymph, back up on the
leader at a distance of, let us say, eighteen inches. That
lets the nymph move lightly and naturally in the twisting
currents at a level just above the streambed. One more
step may be added. Instead of clamping our weight to
the leader, we can hang a twelve-inch section of *fine*
monofilament from a leader knot about eighteen inches
above the nymph and at the bottom of that mono put on
our weight. That gives the nymph even more freedom of
motion and adds the advantage that if our weight is caught
in the rocks we can break it off, losing only the weight
and not the nymph as well.

There's a big problem inherent in fishing with sinking
lines. Because they sink, they're hard to pick up for the
next cast. The sinking line will require the angler to bring
much more line into the guides before he can pick it up
to cast than a floating line will. All that takes time and
effort. You'll tire faster and you'll miss fishing time.
Floating lines are much more pleasant to fish with.

One way of getting a fly down in the water without sacrificing the floating line's longer pickup entirely is to use a *sink tip*. This means that a forward section of the fly line from a few feet to twenty or thirty is sinking line. This sinking line at the tip can give you casting problems. If it is short, it will be a serious break in the tapering of weight from heavy belly to tippet you have worked so hard to accomplish. It may be just as hard to cast as a weighted fly that will get down to the same depth.

If the sink-tip is a long section, then it becomes like a shooting head—which will give greater casting distance and will take the line down swiftly at that point. A short front taper and leader will provide good depth coverage. Shooting heads lack something in delicacy and accuracy but when fishing deep those points are not so important.

Another important factor in deciding how to rig or weight the nymph is the water to be fished. If it is rugged pocket water where the nymph will whisk swiftly by the fish, the unnaturalness of weight in the nymph has less importance and the chance of tangling with the leader on a separate dropper takes on more. Most nymph fishermen, especially in western water, prefer to use weighted nymphs; in the West, most of the nymphs they're imitating are big enough to take care of a fair amount of weight.

Night Fishing

Night is a good time to catch big trout. Big trout have been around a while and have usually learned that there's less human activity on the streams at night. Browns, perhaps because of their heritage, often feed at night. On the northern European streams, sea-running brown trout are fished for almost exclusively at night. On the Stewiake, a slow and deep Nova Scotia river where brown trout have developed a run of up to ten pounds, although anglers knew they were there it wasn't until they began fishing at night that many were caught.

The appeal of night fishing lies in the big fish that can be caught. The disadvantages are that you can't see what you are doing. Wading through tricky water, even though you are familiar with it in the daytime, is an uncertain business. All the delicacy of casting perfectly to the normal trout lies vanishes when you can't see them. Playing a fish when you don't know where the snags are or how the currents move can be exciting but it isn't the same as knowing what you're doing and doing it well.

Accept the limitations and you can be effective and enjoy it. If you know a pool where a big fish has been seen, you can figure out where the best feeding lie will be. This big trout, you'll assume, is in hiding most of the day and only comes out at night to displace the daytime holder of that particular choice feeding spot. You familiarize yourself with the area so that you can come down to the pool at night and know where to stand. You've figured out the angle of your cast by picking out something on the skyline, visible even in the low night light, and you've got a small bump on your line where you put a drop of Pliobond or epoxy, big enough to recognize by the feel but not big enough to affect its smooth flow through the guides. Thus you can fish a given spot in the dark, or a given area. That area can be as far as you're sure you can wade easily. A small flashlight may or may not disturb the trout but it can certainly help if you need it.

Leaders for night fishing need only be fine enough to let a wet fly or streamer swim naturally or a dry fly drift freely. Normally, you'll use larger flies at night to make them more visible. Bass bugs and fly-rod mice are effective for big trout at night. So are streamers; a muddler-type streamer may make a little more commotion and be more readily noticed by a trout than a slimmer fly. Trout can not only see with their eyes as well as an owl can but they can sense an object and its motion by the sensors in their median lines. My best night fishing for bass was on the blackest of nights and with a solid black plug.

When you fish at night you'll recognize the value of the song of the reel. It will tell you how fast your fish is running and how far, where a silent reel can leave you bewildered. The sounds of night fishing are part of its charm. You'll hear the sound of the river and it will seem louder than during the day, perhaps because so many of the birds are silent. Usually, too, the wind has dropped and the lesser sounds like those of the crickets and katy-dids have greater prominence. You'll be in a strangely different world unless or until time gives it familiarity.

You'll remember the night sounds of your first big trout for a long, long time.

We've ranged our trout fishing from top to bottom in simple basics. There are many ways in which these techniques can be varied to achieve greater success. Fly fishing for trout is a personal thing. Any angler may find newer or better ways to achieve his own success. Success, incidentally, does not always mean simply catching the most fish, or the biggest, or even the toughest. It may mean catching them on a particular dry fly or even a particular hook size. As a special challenge, I recently set myself the goal of catching an Atlantic salmon of ten pounds or over on a #28 hook, a hook that will break at a one-pound pull. It took me two seasons and many weeks of fishing during which I caught few fish instead of many. Now that I have done it I will revert to normal-size hooks until, perhaps, a new challenge tempts me.

Many of us prefer to catch fish on a dry fly, finding pleasure in seeing the fish break the surface to get the fly. There is also a great satisfaction to be gained by making a fly yourself, perhaps a new and different pattern, and then proving that a trout will take it. You may elect to fish with a particular fly that a companion assures you will not work, at least on that day or at that time because, in your heart you know it will. You will get past the simple catching of fish and be interested in experimenting not only in the flies you make up or use but also in the techniques of fishing them.

All such experience and experimentation can only help prepare us for new and challenging situations . . . and make us more successful fly fishermen.

11

Playing the Fish

Most people play fish by three simple rules. 1. Keep
the tip up (which means that the bending of the rod will
absorb sudden shocks); 2. keep the pressure on (which
means that you're tiring the fish); and, 3. don't give slack
(lest the hook fall out or lose its grip).

It's good to know the rules but important to know,
also, when to break them. To teach how to play fish at
our school, the first thing we do is to set up some rods
with two-pound and four-pound-test tippets tied to the
corner of the porch. The students are told that rods are
designed to work best when the angle between the rod
butt and the fish doesn't exceed 90°. When a rod is pulled
back to a greater angle, like 135°, it is doubled back on
itself under conditions that make it unstable and much
more likely to break. Within the allowable angle, it is
almost impossible to break a rod. If your rod is bent too
far back, pull in line to bring it down to a good angle.

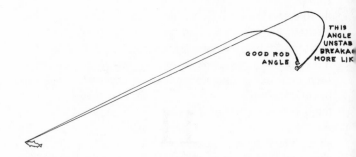

Students find that they have to strain to break a two-pound-test tippet and some don't have the strength to break a four or six-pound tippet by pulling with the rod. Then I ask, do you bend your rod that hard (a pull a little less than the breaking strength) when you play a fish, and, if you don't, why not? This maximum pressure, which few anglers know, can be called the "safe static pressure." It should be applied only when things are static and line is neither going out nor being taken in through the guides. This can happen when neither the fish nor the angler's rod is moving or when both are moving at the same speed in the same direction.

Few fishermen know how hard they can pull with their tackle before it will break, yet knowing that safe pull is one of the most important parts of playing a fish. Therefore, most fishermen, failing to use their tackle to its full power, play fish much too long and endanger the lives of those they intend to release. Every angler should hook his fly to something solid with the varying strength leader tippets he plans to use and learn their strength each season before he starts fishing. Most anglers find this too much trouble. I hope you won't.

The question "How hard?" is especially important when we consider the strike.

What to do when there is a lot of slack in the line and a trout rises to a dry fly, is one such concern. And the only answer can be, try to duplicate the conditions you're thinking of, on a pond or stream. Cast out so that your fly line and leader have in them the amount of slack you want to know about—and then strike, time after time, until you determine exactly how fast and how hard you have to strike in order to make your dry fly move *an inch or two*, just enough to set the point of your hook beyond the barb. When you've found the proper pressure for a particular kind of water, you'll know the answer. And if you'll make these tests with varying amounts of slack, you'll learn how to strike under a wide variety of slack conditions and to strike instinctively with about the right pressure.

One strike that will cut through the most slack is a combination of a haul with the line hand and a move, preferably to the side, by the hand with the rod. A rod is designed to absorb shocks yet a shock is what's needed to set the hook. Line doesn't have any "give" and will transmit a pull right on through its entire length. Lay a piece of rope on the floor. Even if it isn't stretched out in a straight line, if you give a hard yank on one end it will normally be transmitted right on through the entire length to make the far end jump toward you. If it jumps only an inch or two, that is enough to set a hook. It is a good thing to practice to see how much of a pull you need on your line and how much strike with the rod to move your slack-floating dry fly far enough to hook a fish.

With wet flies a strike is not normally required but most of us do lift the rod a bit when we feel the fish to be sure that there's enough pressure given to set the hook. A strike that's too hard will make the hole of the hook's penetration bigger and start the process of weakening the flesh at that point. Many a fish has been lost, many minutes later, without the fisherman's knowing what caused it. Most fishermen strike too hard.

The next question may be, "But exactly how hard should the actual pressure at the hook point be in order to make it sink into the flesh beyond the barb?"

My answer would be, on the next few fish you catch and keep, put hooks of varying sizes into their mouths and pull on your leader to see how hard you have to pull to set the hooks. If you don't keep many or any trout, the next time a leg of lamb is going to be cooked in your kitchen, try sinking the barbs of various hooks into the flesh. Try where it's softest and try where it is toughened a bit by skin or sinew.

Your first reaction may be that this is a lot of trouble. And so it is. Learning takes thought, time, and effort. There is no way an oracle can let you kneel before him (or her) and touch you with his magic wand and give you knowledge of this sort. You have to acquire it and most of it is there to be acquired, in the best way, by working out your own answers.

Many fly fishermen worry about slack. If I bare my forearm and stick a #10 hook into it beyond the barb, how long will it stay there if I don't pull it out? Probably a week. Why, then, do we worry about giving fish slack? Obviously we don't have to worry unless, during the playing, the flesh around the hook's hold has been torn enough to let the hook fall out. Sometimes I will hook some trout in our pond and give them complete slack time after time without losing them. Even barbless hooks will hold when slack is given, *most of the time*, with the smaller ones holding better with slack than the larger ones.

Do I use barbless hooks?

Not often. Mostly when I have to.

Many fishermen today think that if they *don't* use barbless hooks the fish they release will die. But *all* of the fish I return to the water, and there have been thousands, swim away strongly when I release them and I know from many observations that they live. Why, then, must I use barbless hooks to be a good sportsman? Barbless hooks should be your choice, not your necessity or a requirement for being considered a sportsman. Since slack is a tool I can use to play fish faster and barbless hooks

may not let me use it as well without the risk of a lost
fish, the fish I play on barbed hooks can have a better
chance of survival.

Because I have been making movies of fish since 1938,
not just playing them but making them act, making them
jump when I wanted them to, making them run or stop
or rest to give me the particular shots I needed to tell
the story on film, I've learned a great deal about controling fish that most anglers haven't even thought about.
It began in 1938 in Newfoundland with a salmon film I
was making for the Province, which was then a British
Colony. I had an assistant to do photograpy and I was
the actor/angler. We went to a salmon pool with the sun
slanting down on the water at 7:30 in the morning. Ralph
sat on a rock at the side of the pool with the camera ready
to go. Periodically he had to change the lens opening when
clouds covered the sun in varying degrees and to change
the distance setting when I waded farther from shore.
He stayed right on the job. Eight-thirty passed. Then
9:00. At 9:30 he moved over to the lunch box to get a
soft drink. Still no salmon had risen to take the fly.

At 10:00 Ralph went off to the bushes for just a minute
and in that minute I hooked a salmon. It came whirling
out of the water in a magnificent series of leaps and splashes
and my call brought Ralph running back. Again, the salmon
leaped and ran while Ralph looked up at the sun to set
the lens opening and then asked, "Where is he?"

I pointed far down the pool and said, "Near that boulder." Ralph checked the distance setting and aimed the
camera there and when he saw the fish jump started it
running. As I'd advised he kept it running and the second
jump of the fish was captured on film from beginning to
end. The first jump was half over before Ralph had started
the camera and, since it wasn't complete, I knew I wouldn't
use it in the film. We got the landing of the fish in full
detail, changing lenses for a closeup, and following the
fish out to deep water after the release.

We had a good salmon landing on film but we had only

one tired jump, far in the distance. It wasn't fair to the salmon and obviously we wouldn't attract many tourist-fishermen if that was all the action a Newfoundland salmon would give them. I had to think.

I am a salmon. I was born in this stream not far above this pool. I spent four years in this section of the river feeding on its insect life and grew to a six-inch length before drifting down to sea with the spring floods. Then I swam the ocean for thousands of miles, feeding on shrimp and capelin and other good-tasting and nourishing things. I saw whales and sharks and jelly fish. I was chased by seals. I saw cruise ships and rowboats. I saw nets and escaped them. Finally, after two years, during which I'd increased my weight to twelve pounds, I decided it was time to come home. So I looked at the sun and the moon and the stars and felt the swing of the ocean currents and headed back to this, my native river.

I struck the coast some forty miles away and swam along it, smelling the changes in the sea's salinity and poking in toward shore to smell each river. The moment I smelled this one I knew it was mine and came into it full of memories and feeling strange changes within my body. I worked my way upstream, pausing quite a while at a forks where the difference between the two flows was small, until I was sure this was the branch of my birth. Then I swam on up until I came to this pool.

I had a great feeling of being home, of wanting to rest here. I had a feeling, too, of great well being. I was filled with energy and strength. Yet something told me I'd need it all in the times just ahead and as much as possible should be kept in reserve. I hadn't felt any hunger, which was strange and lucky, too, for the salmon parr I'd seen, because they were smaller and easier to catch than the herring and capelin I'd been feeding on out in the salt water.

I must have swum around the pool fifty times, looking it over, before finally picking out a resting place. It was a lie at which I could feel the gentle flow of the stream yet not have to expend much energy to hold my position there. I had sunshine on the bright days to add a little warmth to the river water, which was a little cooler than the sea I'd just left. There was deep water beside me in which I could escape an otter, water deep enough to discourage an osprey. I'd found a great spot for rest and safety.

If some creature, like an eel, otter, or merganser, were to attack me, I'd use all my strength to escape. I'd swim faster than any salmon had ever swam before. I'd leap higher. I'd fight to survive because my instincts were telling me that important times were ahead for me—the best, the most important, days of my life. On the other hand, if a sea louse that had clung to my side when I had come in from the sea were to bite me I'd simply ignore it or, at most, try to scrape that side against a rock to dislodge it.

Just how wildly a salmon can react to danger had come to me dramatically the season before when, on the White Bear River of Newfoundland's south coast, I'd hooked a salmon. I had on a fifteen-pound-test leader and was using a sturdy nine-foot rod. I leaned back at the strike as hard as I dared. The result was electrifying. The salmon, startled and wild, made a leaping run like a sailfish that carried it not only to the far bank but six feet on into the alders that lined it. I left my rod with a rock on it and had to walk a quarter of a mile downstream to find a place shallow enough to cross; then I walked up the far bank to get the salmon, and, carrying it, followed the same course back to where my rod lay.

At any rate, when the next salmon for my movie rose, I simply gave the rod a little twitch to set the hook and then let the line go completely slack. As I'd figured out, the salmon simply drifted back to the preferred place he'd spent so much time choosing. I shouted for Ralph to come beside me. I pointed to a large white rock showing on the streambed and said, "The salmon is just about six feet ahead of that rock. We know where he is, so put on the telephoto lens and set the camera for slow motion." He did this. He pointed the camera at the spot indicated and when I heard it rolling I tightened up on the fish, which then came out in a beautiful series of leaps that were something any Newfoundland salmon could be proud of and that any salmon angler would love to have happen at the end of his own line. That was my first step in making fish act.

My best example of slack at the strike came when I was fishing for a striped marlin record on a fly for ABC's "American Sportsman" series. I hooked the record fish only to hear, over the intercom, "We've got camera problems." I was in a fifteen-foot skiff and I immediately gave slack, following behind the fish as he lazed along in the sun. He didn't know he was hooked. The slight drag didn't bother him because these big fish often have remoras (fish that attach themselves to the marlin and ride along with them until they feed, then feed, too) clinging to their sides which must add a drag similar to my slacked-off fly line.

It was a full five minutes before word came over the intercom that the cameras were ready. Now where was the fish? I reported that the fish was exactly 52 feet in front of the boat, something I could determine by the marks on my fly line. The camera boat came up into position and, when they waved that they were rolling cameras, I leaned back as much as I dared with the twelve-pound-test leader and the result was that the surprised marlin gave us the finest series of marlin jumps ABC ever got.

Slack is a great tool in the playing of a fish. It gives you time and time can be precious. Once, while playing a salmon at the Shellbird Island Pool of the Humber River in Newfoundland I had my reel jam up. I was close to shore and, angling over to it, I set the reel seat firmly into a crotch in an alder so that it would hold and, going back to my car, I drove six miles to the Glynmill Inn where I was staying, got another reel, came back and attached it to the line and landed the seventeen-and-a-half-pounder.

Does that surprise you?

It shouldn't.

Suppose you were alone out on the northern tundra where you can see for miles. You crawl out of your tent in the morning and see a grizzly fifty feet away. He stands up. Then he starts toward you. You run and you hear him breathing behind him so you put everything you have into the effort. You're breathing hard, starting to stagger. After a bit you can't hear him behind you so you take a quick glance back. You see that the bear is running off toward the horizon and there's not another living thing in sight, all around the horizon. What would you do next?

You'd sit down and rest. You'd be thankful that the bear had stopped chasing you and perhaps wonder what it was all about. The last thing you'd do would be to keep on running. Just so with a fish. What's happened to him when he's hooked is inexplicable. When its over, he'll rest where he is or in the nearest convenient place he can find good resting water. You can count on it if he's at all tired.

Drifting down an Oregon river in a McKenzie boat, while making a movie of steelhead fishing I hooked a good fish. The fish went down out of the pool and we followed through the rapids. In the middle of the fast water the cameraman signaled he was out of film. I sang out, "Throw out the anchor." The guide objected, saying we'd lose the fish. I insisted. The anchor went over and we slowed to a stop. The fish ran a short distance, then stopped and waited patiently until the camera was reloaded, and then we all went on down together to the quiet water of the next pool, photographing as we went.

If you have a hooked fish that heads for a snag, don't just try to stop him with a braking power that will break your leader. Let him go. Often a fish will go into a snaggy place and, once there, feel that he's safe until you give him a few line twitches that tell him that he still isn't

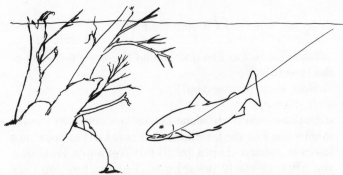

free. If he decides to move to some place else, he's likely to come out of that snag the same way he went in and you can start playing him again. Recently, a fresh-water striper I hooked at Santee Cooper wrapped the line around a sunken branch. I bounced the rod lightly against the line a few times, then firmly, without result, and my companions said I'd have to break the fish off. But I waited a little longer and the fish apparently swung back around the branch, freeing the line and then coming to the boat.

Fish often position themselves near or in a snag or problem foliage. Even though the situation may look impossible, there may be a chance of landing him. If he's a good one, it ought to be worth wasting a fly just in the hope of hooking him. If you can drop a dry fly on a plop cast, with a lot of slack, into a spot where a big fish has taken a lie in under some branches, he may take your fly before the curent tightens the line and sets up an unnatural drag. *Then* you can worry about how to land him.

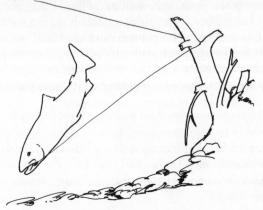

Flies are expendable. When bushes hang down from the far bank over deep water, creating a lie where you know a good trout should be, why not take a chance? Drop your wet fly, nymph, or streamer (one you have a spare for) fairly well upstream of the trailing branches to give the fly a chance to sink a little. Just as it reaches the right spot give it a bit of motion. If you're lucky, you'll either get a strike or have your fly drift on through without getting hung up. If you aren't, you've just lost a fly.

I well remember a situation of that type. A good trout was rising under a low walk-bridge across a feeder of the Bitterroot in Montana. The bridge was ten feet wide, the stream about thirty. The fish was lying in the midpoint in the central flow. I knew I couldn't cast up under the bridge from my position downstream; the bridge was too low to the water. Instead, I cast up *over* the bridge, a long, high cast with a lot of slack, enough to let the fly drift free to the fish. His take and the immediate drag of the current on the leader set the hook. I ran up onto the bridge, reeling in but not putting any pull on the fish until I was at the upstream edge. I played him with my rod held low, to work him up into some quieter water, then moved on down to the stream bank for the release.

Think, when you're playing a fish, about what he can know and what his instinctive reactions will be. That way you can improve on the old rule of "tip up, tight line." Of course, that rule will work, after a fashion. Just how well I used to prove every once in a while at my fly-in salmon camp in northwest Newfoundland. Now and then a couple would come to the camp, bringing along a son or daughter of nine or ten. It was a wilderness camp and we had no nature trails or playing fields and the youngster would get bored. After a few days, I'd go to the parents and ask, "How would you like to have little Augustine catch a salmon?"

Their eyebrows would lift and they'd query, "Little Augustine?"

I'd nod and say, "I think she could manage it. It will cost you five bucks for one guide for one afternoon."

If they were beginners, they'd probably caught only one or two salmon in three days. They'd think a minute and then nod their heads and say, "Okay."

First we'd find out just how far Augustine could cast; this usually wasn't far. We'd give her instructions and put her in the bow of the canoe. The guide would keep shifting the canoe until Augustine—with her steady one-length, one-directional casting—was putting her fly right over a salmon. Every camp operator worth his salt has a few ready fish in special spots saved for paraplegics and politicians and it was to one of those we'd go. In a little while a fish would come up and take the fly and the rod would go down and the reel would scream. Augustine would look at the guide and when the line was slack and she could lift the rod easily, he'd nod and she'd start to reel in. When the line tightened and the rod was pulled down again, she'd take her hand from the reel as if it was red hot and it would scream again. When the fish stopped and she could lift the rod up again easily, she'd reel in again. The minute the fish pulled her rod down, she'd yank her hand from the reel and let him run free. (We'd have her in an open pool, free of snags.) In about fifteen or twenty minutes the tired fish would swim across the guide's submerged net and he'd lift the fish aboard. Playing a fish can be that simple—but most of the time there are problems and solving them can give an angler a great deal of satisfaction.

When I first used small rods many salmon fishermen said that big fish couldn't be played with them. Some insisted, "But you can't really pull hard with them." I'd reply that I could lower my rod and, by moving away, break a hundred-pound line if I wanted to. Then they'd say, "But what do you do when a fish sulks?" I'd reply that my fish didn't sulk if I was free to move. And they'd look at me with disbelief.

If a fish is hanging downstream in the current at just

the right angle from the line, he can put terrific pressure on your tackle. If you took a piece of wood the same size and length as the fish, put a halter on it to give it the right angle, and let it hang in the same spot, it too would put a similar strain on your tackle. The stick is inanimate and doesn't have to spend any energy to hold its position in that flow. Neither does the fish. Hanging there in the current doesn't tire him out. But if the angler moves downstream and the pull comes laterally or from below, the fish has to move. Now he has to fight the current to hold his place in it. If the angler is below him, the fish not only has to fight the current but the pull of the tackle as well. That's tiring. Even though a fish may not be moving, if he is either fighting a strong current or fighting an angler's strong static pressure, he is getting tired fast. By using maximum static pressure on a sulking fish *from downstream*, you can make him move in a matter of minutes. And, moving, he will continue tiring.

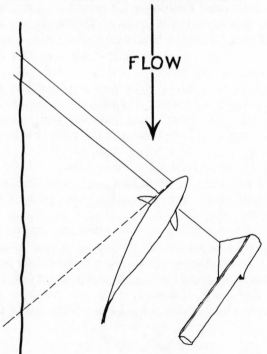

FLOW

Those of us who have played great fish in the sea on light lines realize that our tackle doesn't pull a fish around and tire him out because of his resisting. That can happen with a one-pound trout on a four-pound-test leader but not with a sailfish on a ten-pound-test line or a big trout on a three-pound-test leader. The truth is that the fish tires himself by his own efforts to escape until, when he's tired, the safe static pull of the angler's tackle will move him to net or boatside. Just as with Augustine, smart anglers let the fish tire themselves out without a lot of effort on their own part.

Most of these techniques are important with large rather than small fish. When your leader is twice as strong as a fish's weight, the problem is not really great. It is simply a matter of using the rod's resilience to take up the shock of a sudden surge and give time to get your hand off the reel handle so the fish can run free. But it's the big ones we're most anxious to keep and to play well. Here's the method I use when it's important that I land the fish, not get pictures of jumps or other angling action.

At the rise I'll set the hook with a quick little snap of the rod—then give slack. Sometimes I'll even strip line off the reel to give the fish a chance to settle. Most of the time it is simply a matter of lowering the rod quickly—and I really mean very quickly—as soon as the hook is set. This doesn't come naturally and you may have to work on it. Then the first thing to do is to get rid of the casting slack between the reel and the first guide. I do that by holding the line as it comes in between my first two fingers, let it loop down, and then pass between the third finger and pinkie before going to the reel. If the fish pulls, the line will slide out readily between the first two fingers; meanwhile, as I reel in, the rear fingers will put enough tension on the line to wind it smoothly onto the reel spool. When the loop disappears the fingers are spread and the line is on a direct pull from reel to first guide. It is easy, sometimes, to play a fish by stripping line, letting the loose line fall to the bottom

of the boat or to the water, but any fish I really want to land I play directly from the reel to avoid the embarrassment of having a knot form in the loose line that will catch at the first guide and cost me the fish.

The next considerations are, "Am I in the best position to play this fish? Should I move to shallower water?" If I need to move I'll be doing this while I'm taking out the casting slack, or I'll give slack as I move.

While playing my fish, I will control the drag by relaxing or increasing pressure on the fly line as I hold it back or let it slip through my fingers where they press against it just in front of the reel. The finger pressure gives me instant relaxation or increase of pressure. My reels have a click setting that is just enough to keep them from over-running, no more.

The angle of my rod varies the drag a fish has to pull against to move line. If the rod is pointed directly at a fish, the drag of the guides is at a minimum; I do that when I want a fish to run freely, perhaps on a very light tippet. If I hold my rod up high, the drag of the guides comes to a maximum. Between the angle of my rod and the pressure of my fingers, I can maintain excellent control. If the fly line goes out off the reel and the backing line passes between my fingers, I cannot use finger pressure on it without burning skin. Then I use my left hand to give additional drag by pressing a finger or fingers against the rim, if it is a rim control reel, or against the inside of the outer flange of the reel spool, made bare because the full fly line is off the reel. Using this system, I don't ever get finger burns yet have the best possible drag control on a fish's runs.

Having reached a good playing position, I'll put a little pressure on the fish. It won't be enough to send him off on a wild run but enough to make him uncomfortable and cause him to move a little. The moment the fish starts to move, I'll take off all pressure and let him run freely. He'll move a bit and stop. I tighten up and make him uncomfortable again; then, again he'll make a short run. If I held back hard it would be a long, wild run—which I don't want. Such a run could take him out of the pool or far away where I'd have to play him on a long line with a greater chance of having it foul up somewhere along the way. About the third or the fourth time that I make him uncomfortable, he'll realize that he's really in trouble and will put his heart into his effort to get away. But by that time he will not be as wild as if I'd pressured him at first. He'll be a bit used to the strange pressure on his jaw. He'll be a little out of breath from the short dashes he's already made. He'll be more docile than when he was first hooked. Then you work on him as much as your tackle will let you. Use static pressure when you can. Otherwise, use enough pressure to make him move in tiring moves. A few good runs and leaps and I'll find times when I can apply more static pressure. He'll grow tired.

A fish will resist being pulled to the stream bank as energetically as you would resist being pushed into a pool of sulphuric acid. He doesn't *want* to come into the air at the shore. If you'll wade out to a depth of water in which he's comfortable, two feet or more, you can control him much more easily. You can have a fish make a complete circle around you, then—and work at any angle in all 360°. You'll bring him to net or hand that much quicker, which will, in turn, give him that much better chance of survival if you're going to release him.

A fish to be released can be corralled in a net so that he can be unhooked without lifting him from the water or holding him with any squeezing pressures. Perhaps the best release is simply to grip the shank of the fly with longnosed pliers or a hemostat and remove it without ever touching the fish, either while corralled in the net or played to a point where you can reach the hook without a net. Beaching fish is effective if you're going to keep them; they have to be tired enough to be kept headed up onto the beach and unable to turn aside until grounded; then, with a moderate pull, their own efforts will drive them up farther since they're not designed to back up well.

There is a second side to playing fish beyond just tiring

them out. That is the psychological. If you can destroy their will to fight, you can subdue them more quickly. That's the reason why I let fish run on a completely slack line. They think they're free. They've just made a great effort and, suddenly, the pressure is gone. They swim a ways and relax. Then that pressure comes back again, telling them that they're not free. Each effort they make is more desperate and each time its failure hurts more. Finally they give up. They've been able to do their best and it wasn't good enough. You can break a horse. You can train a dog. You can break a fish's spirit, too.

Contrast these pressures with a steady pulling of the fish. Then the fish settles into a tug-of-war and keeps right on tugging until he's completely exhausted. Such fish have the least chance of survival. Tug-of-wars take a lot more time.

An important factor in playing fish is to remember from which side you hooked them. Since fish are almost always heading upstream, you'll know which side that is. If, during the playing of the fish, you find you've changed sides, play with minimal pressure. The illustration shows how a change of direction can use the shank length of the hook as leverage to tear the flesh at its hold and help it tear free or work out.

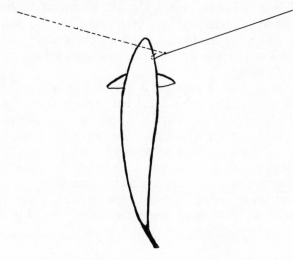

Another important factor in playing fish is the amount of line out. Line has a friction when pulled through the water and it can build up with increasing current and increased length. Much as your guide may want to leave the canoe at anchor, when you're out into your backing, it's best to follow the fish. If you're on foot follow him. Get line back. You can con fish into swimming toward you when they're still strong *sometimes* but it isn't worth losing a good fish because you were too lazy to follow him or the guide was too lazy to move the canoe.

An important trick with such big fish as steelheads, when they're in a pool or run and you don't want them to go down through the fast water at the tail, is to *walk* them upstream. I cannot explain why this technique works so well but can assure you that it does. A tired fish, if you can get him to stop and rest above the tail rapids, can almost always be persuaded to move along a little with a steady pull. Start with light pressure and increase it *very* gradually until the fish starts to move. Then, maintaining that same pressure, walk upstream at a slow and steady pace. The fish will come along, I believe, because the pressure is steady. If you try to reel in so that *you* won't have to move, the pressure on the fish will be jerky because of your reeling and he'll come only a little way before he'll run again. The movement of the line caused by reeling, or by a quivering of the rod, will cause most quiet fish to run. But a steady pressure has walked a good many fish back up into quiet waters for an easy landing.

 I've often heard it said that a fish *must* be kept in the pool if he is to be landed. That isn't always true. I've saved a lot of fish that went down into the heavy, rough water below such pools. Again, the important word is slack. Let them go. Wise anglers carry enough backing line on their reels to manage this. Complete slack should be given so there is no nagging pull to urge them on. A fish that has ascended a river on a spawning run can well ask himself, "What am I going downstream for? I just came up!"

As soon as they come to a good resting place, most fish will stop, perhaps to rest. The current will carry the slack line downstream behind them. It will usually hang up on the rocks and whatever else is causing the rough water. An angler following along can reel in and clear the line of these objects as he follows. More often than not, when the angler reaches the fish he'll still be on, resting there and perhaps doing a little wondering. Renewed pressure may send him off on another downstream run, particularly if he's too tired to want to buck his way up through the rough water just then. Again, the angler can follow his slack-running fish perhaps through two or three more stops until the fish reaches water quiet enough for a landing. How much better that is than to have held too hard and broken tackle in an effort to hold the fish in the pool.

On western streams, I've had good rainbows make a long run then go into overhanging bushes or willow roots along a bank. Once the fish starts his run he is on complete slack. When he goes into the snag, I walk toward him, reeling in but without any tension on the line. I've reached a place outside the snag and sometimes seen the fish. Sometimes he'll come out where he went in; occasionally he'll go out through some other passage. If there is no pressure, the line will simply follow along behind him. There's no drag or pressure to break a tippet or pull out a hook. And sometimes I've been able to pass my rod in the path of the line on through the snag to the other side where the fish went out and play and land him in the open water beyond. Once a rainbow took my line between two big rocks that just touched under two feet of water. Again, it was complete slack and passing the rod through the passage the fish had taken that let me keep him on and land him. Slack can be wonderful.

Playing a fish is a lot like driving a car in a road race. You can drive just so fast without going off the road on the curves and you can hold or pull just so hard without breaking your tackle. Playing time with given tackle is a measure of one's skill. It is satisfying to play fish well, particularly if the fish is to be released. The longer a fish is played the slimmer his chances of survival. Knowing that safe "static" pull and using it on a tiring fish is a key to survival for released fish.

If you *do* tire a fish out completely, hold him, headed upstream and upright, in a current to revive him. I've been saddened to see people pushing an exhausted fish forward and backward through the water, time after time. Pushing him forward *helps* him to breathe. Pulling him backward *chokes* him. If you can't find a reasonable flow to head him into, push him forward through the water continuously. If a straight line isn't possible, make a big circle.

An angler can take a special pride if, whenever he unhooks a fish to release it, it swims away strongly on its own. This can be managed no matter how fine the leader point or how large the fish.

That's part of the measure of the angler.

Good Luck!

Y ou have studied the trout and the streams in which he lives. You have studied the available tackle and perhaps made a few improvements of your own. You've learned to make or buy interesting flies that will catch trout for you and you've learned to bring in big trout on the fine leaders it sometimes takes to fool them. You've become a fine trout fisherman. What's next?

Fly fishing for trout is a forever thing. It is you and clean, flowing water. It is you, inquisitive, in a wild world that is older than man, seeking greater understanding and finding not only an endless interest but a tranquility that comes, most of the time, to all nature's wild creatures, be they predators or prey. On a trout stream, perhaps, an angler is most fully alive.

In 1937 I wrote: "A good game fish is too valuable to be caught only once. It is the finest gift one angler can give another and, who knows, that trout you just caught may have been some other angler's gift to you."

That still seems like a philosophy for wise trout fishermen to live by.

Index